DON'T RIDE A DINOSAUR

INTO YOUR BATTLE FOR NEW CLIENTS

AND OTHER LESSONS FOR LEADERS WHO WANT TO GROW THEIR BUSINESS

JEFF ANTAYA

Getting the Best Out of Your Marketing and Business Development Team in a Professional Services Firm

The marketing field is changing fast. To be competitive, you have to innovate — after all, that's what your competitors are doing!

You know you can't ride a dinosaur into battle, but where do you start? This book is intended to help leaders in professional services firms who aren't marketing professionals better understand the best practices to grow their firms and work with their marketing and sales team members to achieve that growth. Marketers may also find it useful to help educate their teams and the partners they work with every day.

I've organized this book into bite-sized chapters. You can read from front to back in one sitting, or you can use the content in each chapter as it becomes relevant to your situation. Your choice.

Enjoy!

Table of Contents

Section Five: If It Were Easy, Everyone Would Do It   191

My Last Word.   241

APPENDIX   245

DON'T RIDE A DINOSAUR

INTO YOUR BATTLE FOR NEW CLIENTS

AND OTHER LESSONS FOR LEADERS WHO WANT TO GROW THEIR BUSINESS

JEFF ANTAYA

Acknowledgments

Passion gives life to possibility! "Don't Ride a Dinosaur into Battle" was first sparked by a couple of sessions with Jim Giszczak and Miriam Rosen from McDonald Hopkins. The needs they expressed kept ringing in my ears, so I sat down to transfer as much of my knowledge as possible to the written page in hopes that my expertise can help others.

This book wouldn't have been possible without my 13-year career at Plante Moran and my ongoing discussions with each of the managing partners to whom I reported. In my time at the firm, I spent almost 1,000 hours collectively with Bill Hermann, Gordon Krater, and Jim Proppe. Their encouragement drove my desire to help Plante Moran leapfrog our competition by shining a bright light on the wonderful partners, staff, and clients that made Plante Moran the powerhouse professional services firm and cultural leader it's become.

As I finished the first draft, many colleagues and friends invested their time to read my manuscript and provide feedback. This group included:

Brian Blaha,
Growth Partner, Wipfli, LLP

Joan Budden,
Past President, Priority Health

Tom Doescher,
President, Doescher Advisors

David Foltyn,
Managing Partner,
Honigman LLP

Bill Hermann,
Managing Partner
Emeritus, Plante Moran

Ed Hogikyan,
Founder, EAH

Terry Kerscher,
Business Development
Leader, Wipfli

Christine Kloostra,
Executive Director, Marketing
and Communications, DIA

Gordon Krater,
Managing Partner
Emeritus, Plante Moran

Dave Maney,
Founder & CEO, Deke Digital

Leslie Murphy,
President,
Murphy Consulting

Suzanne Reed,
CMO, LBMC

Peter Rosenfeld,
Senior Advisor, BCG

Roy Sexton,
Marketing Director, Clark Hill

Bill Sullivan,
Founder, Bill Sullivan Enterprises

Rana Taylor,
Director of Communications,
ACCESS

Frank Troppe,
Sales Consultant, Korn Ferry

I especially want to thank Bill Hermann for really investing in this project. His help has been invaluable. Bill gave me the constructive feedback that was essential to transform the manuscript into a book. If that wasn't enough, he volunteered to write my foreword. I'm eternally grateful to this man who so many of us admire more than words can express.

As my work progressed, I was fortunate for all of the wonderful editorial assistance of my Plante Moran colleague and friend, Teresa McAlpine. She served as editor, coach and motivator. She got me over the finish line.

This book was also the beneficiary of help from some key individuals who brought design, editing, and polish that wouldn't have been possible without them. Thank you to Amanda Dine, Mindy Kroll, Andrew Patterson, and Tracy Turner.

Lastly, to you, my readers: Thank you for being my inspiration! You helped fuel the passion that made this book possible.

Now, let's get started.

Foreword:
From pencils to pixels — a marketing evolution

By Bill Hermann, Plante Moran
Managing Partner Emeritas

"There's never enough time for business development."

— Anonymous professional services firm partner

My very first experience with marketing came in 1971 as a proofreader at CPA firm Plante Moran. The office manager got a great buy on navy blue No. 2 pencils, an essential tool of the trade at the time, and the pencils were inscribed with the name of the firm in gold letters. Unfortunately, the state Board of Accountancy didn't allow "advertising" by accounting firms and the pencils were deemed a violation of professional ethics. Plante Moran was ordered to destroy the pencils or face a fine or worse. Determined not to waste money, our thrifty office manager sent us to the hardware store to buy No. 2 sandpaper. We spent several afternoons sanding the firm's name off thousands and thousands of brand-new pencils.

Fortunately, times have changed and the rules governing our ability to present our capabilities to clients and prospects have softened considerably. Not only can we put our names on a pencil, it's digital pixels that make up the images on our websites, emails, and online communications. Organizations now have access to systems, tools, and digital capabilities that could not have been imagined 50, 30, or even 20 years ago. If you're interested in growing your organization, this book will let you know what some of those tools are and how you can use them to grow.

The evolution in marketing and business development has been swift. In this book, Jeff Antaya is our guide to the present state of marketing capabilities. Jeff offers a terrific blend of perspective, suggestions, marketing tools, and the questions you should ask if you're ready to move ahead with your marketing efforts. His deep experience will challenge you to consider approaches that may be foreign but will improve your marketing focus and your results.

Everyone wants a vibrant organization that will provide opportunities for personal growth and financial security. Not only do businesses have to grow the top line, it's estimated that most firms must replace as much as 25% of their revenue every year. There are lots of reasons for this: the vagaries of business — companies go out of business, they sell, the owners may die, non-recurring one-time projects are completed. Someone needs to create demand for those services that will lead to growth, and that's the role that marketing will deliver.

New approaches for today's world

The world has changed and so has the value equation for clients. It used to be that professional service organizations could sustain themselves simply through technical knowledge of their discipline, strong personal relationships, and focused client service. Not only has online technology revolutionized marketing's evolution, it's added additional hurdles to those relying only on traditional factors. The internet has opened the eyes of the purchaser to capable options they never knew existed.

Today, thought leadership begins to influence prospects way before the buying cycle ever begins and, by the time the traditional buying process gets under way, many organizations have already decided on who they want to work with and the RFP is a formality. Obviously, technical knowledge is still critical for professional service organizations to sustain themselves, but the firm who makes a good first impression may have the upper hand. Clients today are often using published thought leadership as the measurement of a firm's ability to help them. Published thought leadership demonstrates your experience, insights, and the wisdom that will help them solve their business issues.

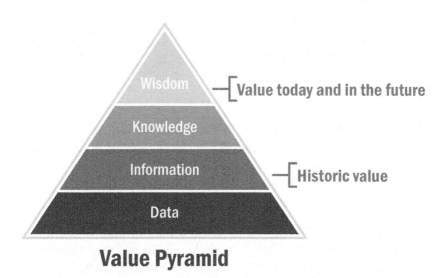

Value Pyramid

Today's formula builds on traditional skills and introduces new wave marketing concepts including thought leadership and leveraging digital technology to improve the effectiveness of your marketing efforts and increase your results if you are willing to take a chance and try something new.

Traditional methods
- Technical competence
- Strong personal relationships
- Focused client service

Meaningful Growth

New wave concepts
- Digital marketing skills
- Thought leadership

The makeup of the individual elements in this formula can vary based on where your organization stands in its marketing evolution. Fortunately, Jeff recognizes that there's no "one-size-fits-all" plan that works for everyone. The best marketers know each organization is unique, and "cookie-cutter" approaches won't differentiate your organization in your appeal to new and existing clients. The time, focus, and resources you choose to apply will depend on the size of your organization, the availability of your marketing staff, and their skill set.

I have often thought that the key to a thriving organization requires leaders and team members with a mindset that is innovative in thought, principled in intent, and intentional in action. Jeff has identified plenty of ideas to seed your innovative thoughts, and he has wrapped these ideas in practical, value-focused action steps. He didn't leave you alone to figure all this out: He's offering multiple tools that can be used to create effective and measurable action plans.

The rate of change that we thought was mind-blowing years ago is speeding up daily. We find ourselves in a world where there's less time to do more. In order to keep up and even advance, it requires collaboration between practice leaders and marketing staff to create a cohesive effort to gain potential clients and expand services with existing clients. No one really knows what will happen when you take a chance, but it's guaranteed that nothing will happen if you decide to sit on the sidelines and do nothing. By deferring action, you may put your organization at a competitive disadvantage.

It's been my experience that many partners in professional service firms see business development as a burden that takes time away from client service. They may also say, "I didn't go to school to become a salesperson." This book will go a long way to modify those perceptions and may be exactly the encouragement that you need to change your approach and take advantage of the new resources that await when you're ready to jump on board.

— Bill Hermann, June 2021

Preface

Do better

I recently read that, when most of us are faced with a decision, our natural instinct is to select the status quo and opt for the familiar versus trying something new. In many cases, it's easier to stick with marketing and business development practices we've been using for years — even as we realize they're not as effective as they once were.

As the kid who was raised in a household of modest means, I realized early on that the status quo wasn't enough for me. I was fortunate that my parents wanted more for me as well, and while college wasn't in my parent's story, they insisted that it was a necessity for their four children.

The intention to do better is powerful, and it allowed me to create manageable pieces to my future. I remember teaching myself to do my dad's taxes so I could complete the required financial aid forms. My focus, curiosity, and energy were stoked by the success I achieved. That's not to say that everything fell into place perfectly, but I've always had my mind focused on a better future — and trying new things and improving on past results were part of the journey. This open-mindedness about the unknown and relentless search for what's new, improved, or innovative helped to fuel any success I ever had. If you've picked up this book, my guess is that you may be open to this as well.

Whether you prefer the tried and true or the next big thing, there's no debating that companies that tap into new and potentially disruptive ideas are energizing business innovation. Unexpected leaps with technology have made entire sectors obsolete almost overnight. Marketing also has been transformed by technology — look no further than the personalized content and ads that you receive on your devices. Though these advances may be slow to hit certain fields, the changes are coming.

In business, personal relationships have traditionally played a significant role in winning new work. It's possible that strong rainmakers have masked this evolution — maybe giving their organizations a false sense of security. But these same organizations likely also realize they're behind their competitors in the battle for new revenue — and that they're figuratively "riding a dinosaur" when their competitors have upgraded to a Tesla.

Sticking with the status quo may limit success with clients, donors, and referral sources and, ultimately, jeopardize survival. It may also result in unanticipated mergers because leaders discover that they missed the chance to make the investments required for independence, and the cost to catch up is too steep.

In this book, we'll explore the current marketing systems deployed by leading firms that are serious about growth, market share, and legacy. These organizations understand that their competitive advantage in the future will be powered by their client servers, reputation, astute marketing team members, technology processes and, lastly, their data.

You may be wondering, however: who am I to talk to you about leading your team to accomplish these goals? How do I know anything about building an integrated marketing system to achieve the growth you want to accomplish?

Let me introduce myself

By now, you know that my name is Jeff Antaya, and I recently launched a strategic marketing consulting business for professional service firms, wealth management firms, not-for-profit organizations, and many other B-to-B businesses. Prior to that, I enjoyed a 30-plus-year career in accounting, sales, and marketing. I've also had the honor to consult with a few legal firms and been an advisor to some not-for-profit organizations where I served as a board member.

In my 13-year career at Plante Moran — one of our country's top accounting, tax, consulting, and wealth management firms — I worked hand-in-hand with firm leaders to build a marketing system known for challenging the status quo and a steel-like focus on firm growth. I helped the firm grow in each business unit and every customer segment and service line until I retired in 2020.

When I joined the firm in 2007, I was a "boomerang" to the profession. That's because I started my career in 1981 at Price Waterhouse and spent 11 years as an auditor for middle-market companies. This was a great place to learn about client service, cross-serving, and all of the elements of being a successful client server in a professional services organization.

I next moved into two corporate controller positions before I shifted into a completely new role as general sales manager for a startup, Nextel Communications, in 1995. Against great odds, this CPA flourished in the world of sales and marketing. As the general manager for the state of Michigan, my team was always ranked in first, second, or third place in sales leadership nationwide. As a startup organization battling two established carriers, we had to work smarter and harder. We didn't have the budgets of our competitors, so we had to be more creative. The position fueled my affinity for continuous process improvement and instilled in me the leadership skills necessary for exemplary growth. Many of these same skills would later help me at Plante Moran.

In 2007, I was looking for my next challenge, and Plante Moran was looking for a CMO. Despite my roots at Price Waterhouse, my background working in sales at a tech company deviated from the norm of what the firm expected in a successful candidate. Twenty-three interviews later, I received an offer to be the CMO at Plante Moran with the promise of a partner position if things went well. I accepted the challenge, and in 2011, I became the first marketing partner and CMO at Plante Moran — perhaps my greatest accomplishment.

What led to that success? I committed to trying new things and worked tirelessly to innovate in a way that would differentiate us from our competitors — so that decision makers at prospect organizations had to pay attention to Plante Moran. Along the way, I read countless articles, attended many conferences, talked to most vendors who called, took every meeting offered on technology, followed up with people I met at conferences, and built relationships with my peers and beyond. I encouraged my team members to do the same. I knew our future success would largely be found outside our firm. Piece by piece, these activities helped me build an integrated growth strategy that had proven success.

Despite whatever talents I think I had, the real catalyst to my success was the first managing partner I reported to at the firm, Bill Hermann. We shared a vision of what a successful integrated marketing/growth initiative would look like for our firm, and his trust propelled me to do better. It gave me the confidence to build a bridge to our marketing future.

Bill's actions were a roadmap for anyone who wants to motivate their marketing team and help their firm in the process. This is what he did. (If you're a C-suite leader, take note!)

- He respected my marketing expertise and supported me 100% of the time.

- He kept me focused on firm growth and initiatives to support the growth. Nothing was done for branding or positioning if it didn't have an impact on growth.

- He met with me monthly, and we spent at least 90 minutes sharing questions and opinions with each other. (We both came with an agenda.)

- He integrated me into important firm activities where the management team was focused. I was involved in mergers, staff issues, and high-profile topics from the start.

- He gave me a piece of paper where he'd written "NO" in large letters along with his signature with the directive to use it when someone wanted me to use marketing resources for something that didn't make sense to me.

- He gave me the tools I needed to be successful with the partnership and advised me on what didn't matter.

Bill was followed by two other managing partners: Gordon Krater and Jim Proppe. Together, these three men gave me the hands-on education of a lifetime. They gave me confidence and encouraged me to find the ingredients we needed to help the firm grow. I knew that they wanted me to offer new ideas, technologies, and options to increase our growth trajectory. Not all my ideas worked, but there was great learning from those failures. And, fortunately, my ideas worked more often than not.

Jump in!

What I'm proposing will require change! It will mean some additions, some subtractions, and probably more than a few adjustments to some traditional marketing tactics you may have learned in school. But in the new digital world, each element works together to produce a measurable ROI. Everything is connected.

No matter where you are in your use of technology or where your firm falls on the size or marketing budget spectrum, just "jump in." Marketing isn't one size fits all, so you can customize these elements to best meet your firm's needs.

My goal is that you take away at least five new ideas from this two-three hour read and that you value the time spent as you would a marketing MBA — but without the term papers!

Introduction

The phrase, "tip of the iceberg" is commonly used to describe a situation where what we're seeing is just a small part of the whole. It's often a warning that an issue may be more complex than what first meets the eye. (In the case of the *Titanic*, the ship's captain underestimated the magnitude of the iceberg, and overestimated the ship's defenses.)

This book sheds light on individual marketing elements that, when combined in a plan tailored for your firm, will supercharge your growth efforts. Like an iceberg, an integrated plan is much stronger than any standalone elements — yet many of the most powerful tools are out of the sight of the casual observer. To get the full impact, you'll want to embrace both the tools above and below the surface, especially newer digital tools.

You may be thinking, "I don't work at an accounting firm, so why am I reading this book?" The answer is simple: because it wasn't written solely for accounting firms. This book applies to all professional service firms — law firms, consulting firms, architecture firms, and more. Wealth management firms and not-for-profit organizations can easily adapt these strategies to build their client base as well.

This book is designed to be a two-to-three-hour, MBA-level resource in growing your firm. You'll be able to apply these lessons — no matter your organization's size — and in the end, you'll understand how to be more effective marketers and, to quote a classic movie, "what's behind the curtain."

In the preface, I described my journey and touched on several elements of the successful marketing strategy we employed at Plante Moran. However, our transition to a full digital strategy wasn't complete until we recognized the power of integration:

- Learning how the different techniques and technologies we were exploring could work together as one total system.

- Having a team that knew the elements to digital success and how to achieve them while also doing our best to be inclusive of everyone at the firm in a way that aligned with the firm's goals.

Individual marketing tactics — like a web ad, a piece of thought leadership, a radio ad, and a newspaper article — have much more power when linked together as an end-to-end campaign. No single tactic is as powerful to get new business as the collective whole. Growth won't happen as quickly or robustly when tactics are executed one at a time. Throughout the book, I'll demonstrate the power of integration.

I'll also lay a foundation for good marketing and practice development (sales) strategies. The book is broken into several areas; you might use it as a reference for specific topics, or you may read it from cover-to-cover. This material is for anyone who's open to adopting new options for growth. Not everything I offer will resonate with everyone, and some approaches will have to be adjusted, but I hope it inspires deeper thought on the topic of growth. I also hope it will be beneficial to my marketing colleagues who want a seat at the leadership table.

If marketing and sales aren't your natural comfort zone, in my humble opinion, this is the best two to three hours you can invest to become a more confident leader.

What's Ahead, You Ask?

The book is broken into a several sections. In Chapters 1 through 3, we start with some basics. You may have had exposure to some of the ideas, but I urge you to take the time to read these short chapters start to finish, because they're a foundation for the rest of the book.

Once we move past the fundamentals, we'll talk about how to resource your marketing efforts. Rome wasn't built in a day, and your plan may take time to execute; however, that doesn't mean you can't get the help you need to start. In Chapters 4, 5, and 6, we'll look at hiring marketing leadership and how to develop equitable compensation plans for sales executives.

Starting in Chapter 7, you'll hear about the framework for the tactics involved in a good marketing plan — the ones you should be considering and how a group of tactics can complement one another for the best results. We'll start with a discussion about technology and topics that weren't even relevant just 10 years ago but, today, are the core of notable marketing efforts.

In Section Four, we will revisit some of the traditional marketing tactics and see how they have changed. Lastly, in Section Five we will revisit several familiar topics with a common-sense approach for today's business leaders.

Finally, I also include a number of real-world examples taken from my time at Plante Moran. I hope you find these helpful and inspiring in your own journey.

This is not a "how-to book" but a book for leaders who want to improve. After you've finished, you'll be able to recognize the brilliance of a good marketing plan and just as easily identify a weak plan, well before disappointment about results materializes. And you'll be equipped with the tools to be a supportive leader for your marketing team.

I can tell you from firsthand experience, my partners who were nurturing with their marketing support team members and who worked to understand the marketer's point of view got much better support than those who took a "know-it-all" attitude or were unresponsive. Not only will you have an overall knowledge of a roadmap to best meet your firm's needs, but you'll also be motivating the very people who can help get you there. Lastly, you may even pick up a tip to share with a client and increase your standing in their eyes, too.

As you finish each chapter, you'll find a conclusion and ideas to consider for improvement (which I'm calling "Get Off of That Dinosaur") to help emphasize important takeaways. Hopefully, at the end of the book, you'll have a better idea of what your firm's end goal will look like and a few tactics to get you started on the journey. My journey at Plante Moran took almost 13 years, and each step was built on the last. The important thing is to take the first step, keep your goals in mind, and follow a plan of process improvement.

PLAN, IMPLEMENT, EVALUATE, IMPROVE, PLAN...

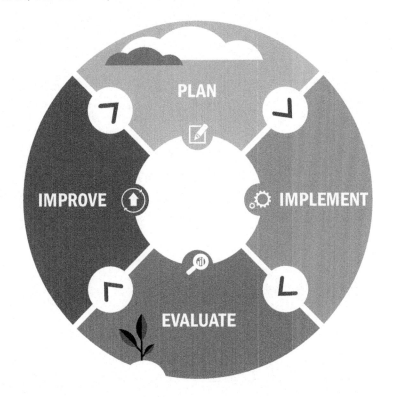

Enjoy the book!

Section One:
The ABCs of Marketing

We all know that the alphabet is fundamental to constructing words and learning to read. We've followed this process with our kids, grandkids, nieces, and nephews. As their vocabulary matures, there's even more dependence on the fundamentals to pronounce new words correctly and make connections with other words to derive possible meaning. But even quick learners can get stumped — and sometimes a short refresher can unlock more potential, even though it may seem like a step backward at the time.

In these first three chapters, we want to review a couple of the fundamentals that are key to achieving the most successful marketing and business development programs. You may already know some of this, but please stick with me. There may be a few, more advanced, thoughts interspersed that will be helpful later in this book.

1

The Road to Winning New Business is Paved With Intentionality.

Really great things happen when we're intentional. When I trained to run a half marathon, I followed a strict 24-week program that helped me build my endurance and enabled me to run farther than I ever imagined.

Good marketing is much the same. It's dependent on intention and planning, just like running. However, the two aren't equally weighted. Intentionality grounds us in the desire to achieve a new goal. It provides the fuel, even when we're feeling depleted. Armed with our intention to change, we can begin.

Our journey to the most advanced marketing methods begins with a more intense focus on our sellers, so let's begin by reviewing the most common ways that we get new business. Like astute investors, smart growth agents don't put all of their eggs in one basket; instead, they intentionally diversify. Financial advisors coach us to have the discipline to invest in multiple asset classes and to have a balanced portfolio commensurate with our age and long-term goals. When working on a growth strategy, a plan that includes multiple resources to recruit new clients and win additional revenue from existing clients provides the greatest chance of success.

In a professional services organization or wealth management firm, marketing strategies might be focused on these avenues for winning new business:

If you're a not-for-profit organization, your targets may look different to increase donations, but the same focus applies. Foundations, corporations, and high-net-worth individuals might be the way you focus your efforts.

Audience segmentation: One size fits one

Segmentation is a fundamental marketing approach that allows marketing efforts to be more client-focused, thereby leading to growth. When organizations segment their target audiences, they're better able to focus their efforts and track how well their message and approach resonate with the target. Rather than using a one-size-fits-all approach to present the case for your firm, segmenting gives you the ability to refine the message and the tools based on exactly who you're trying to reach.

For example, referral sources may be an important target audience, or channel, but it's a big bucket. Segmenting referrals into smaller subsets may make targeting more specialized and will potentially have a greater impact. If law firms are a great source of referrals, grouping their attorneys in distinct segments, such as estate attorneys, intellectual property attorneys, etc., is a way to segment how your firm will talk to each group. What employment law attorney wants to receive a marketing email about cost segregation strategies? Similarly, in a not-for-profit organization, significant audiences are different and would have separate efforts focused on individuals, foundations, and corporate giving because the messaging and tools aren't all the same.

As organizations grow, become more sophisticated, and develop discrete segments, the term "channel" may take on new meaning. A channel may refer to a broader audience (client servers, referral sources, business developers), or it may be defined by the various types of clients (existing clients, family businesses, corporations, private equity owned) with whom you work. In these larger segmentations, more micro-segments may still occur if the additional effort is warranted based on the ROI. Marketing tactics like email, webinars, and personalized web content would apply to each new client acquisition work stream and can be tailored when appropriate.

Like any good diversification strategy, some groups might be focused on the same types of clients, and some may be focused on different types of clients — all with the intention of finding the best way to connect with audiences who have diverse styles and tastes. The segmentation is customized to fit what's right for your organization and only makes sense when the incremental effort to provide a more tailored approach has the right return for the investment.

Regardless of how you segment your target audience, all roads begin with being proactive in defining those segments and understanding

27

their needs. While high performance marketing teams tailor messages depending on the audience, which we know is the single best way to differentiate a firm, what about the business developers, referral sources, existing clients, or other organizational leaders who are out there interacting with prospects? If those people treat everyone the same, your marketing efforts may be in vain — and your ability to be unique is negated.

So, what to do? How can you equip the various people who may be introducing your organization to new prospects with what they need to make the introduction that's consistent with your goals and brand? You partner with your marketing team to create a toolkit that tailors your approach based on three things:

- Target market
- The perspective or issues of prospects within that market
- A customized approach that considers where the prospect is in the buying process

Referral Sources Are People, Too

Referral sources are an important channel to identify new clients and donors, yet there's a unique aspect for engaging them that you may be missing, keeping you from getting a full return of the time you've invested. Consider this: when you send referral sources material, do you (a) direct it to the end prospect, (b) direct it at them — communicating why your firm is worthy of referrals, or (c) both?

The right answer is (c). Directing material to the end prospect is a no-brainer, but that's not enough. No one wants to jeopardize a client relationship with a bad referral, considering referral sources need to have confidence that you'll do a great job. You might even consider developing a referral-focused marketing piece that reassures them that you'll take good care of their clients and not jeopardize their relationships.

To put this two-track approach into motion, you'll need:

- Material that demonstrates how your firm will take great care of their clients — and why their clients won't be disappointed by their referrals
- Material that will speak for itself when the referral source hands it to their client. This content should make clear that you're a great firm with a client focus. It should sell you! (After all, you don't know if the referring party is talking to their clients about you or simply handing over your material.)

One last thought that might be a powerful catalyst to activating referral sources: Can you share with them some organizations you'd like to have as clients? This may transform a more casual encounter into one with intentionality and definition.

Integrate business developers in the pursuit process

Some of you have in-house business developers, and we'll spend time in Chapter 6 on how to fully engage them. However, I'd like to note that business developers are similar to referral sources in several ways. They aren't client servers, and they weren't raised in your firm. To be successful, business developers need background on your client service ratings, how you onboard a new client, and what your firm's quality program looks like. It won't be enough to arm them with your service offerings and the tell-tale signs that your services are needed; they need to have the same confidence in your firm's ability as referral sources do.

Summary

Intentional marketing means being committed to understanding the journey that transitions a prospect to a client — and tailoring a marketing system to significant prospects that resonates with them every step of the way.

In successful organizations, a one-size-fits-all approach to revenue growth has changed to one size fits one. Messages and approaches are tailored to the intended audience. In some cases, it may be tactic-based with personalized emails or special offers. In others, it may be the contact point, perhaps an attorney or other trusted advisor. Lastly, it may be a strategically assembled team of partners who approach the target.

Making sure that whomever approaches the prospect has tailored talking points and materials will result in the best success. Some channels like referral sources may need more than a description of the services you provide; they may also require some material about why they should hitch their wagon to yours versus your competitors.

Engaging everyone in the pursuit of a new client in an individualized way is the difference between a riding a dinosaur and driving a Tesla.

GET OFF OF THAT DINOSAUR!

These questions will help you get out of The Stone Age and into The Digital Age. Ask yourself:

- What segmentation, if any, makes the most business sense for your organization?

- Do your referral sources feel valued and know why they should refer work to you versus your competition?

- Have you given your business developers a full background on your client experience? Can they articulate that premium experience to your prospects?

- How do you judge how effective your customized sales material is performing for your organization?

- Do you have a formal program to reward your highest referral sources?

- Do key referral sources, existing clients, and business developers know your targets?

See Tool 1 in the appendix for items to share with referral sources and business developers.

2

Fire, Ready, Aim:
Who Are Your Ideal Buyers?

My niece just sent me her resume. She's starting the search for her second job after college. She still had the generic one-size-fits-all resume approved by college placement offices across the country, but that won't work for her second job unless she's willing to take whatever's offered.

With a year under her belt, she knows the kind of position that would make her the happiest, so she needs to tell the hiring specialist what she wants and why she's best qualified for that position. This will also be essential to share with anyone she's networking with because they need to know what she wants to be able to help her.

Just like my niece has an ideal job, professional service firms have ideal clients. As leaders, it's our job to paint the picture of those clients — to spell out the details as clearly as possible. By doing this, we create a shared focus for everyone with growth responsibilities. It gets everyone on the same page and, while not every service area may have the same criteria, the exercise of defining the targets and getting to know as much as possible about them will be a rewarding experience.

Previously, the criteria professional service firms used to describe targets was basic:

- Industry
- Size
- Geography

It was a common practice to pull a Dunn & Bradstreet list for the SIC codes for the focus industries and geographies. Armed with a list, we'd send a generic mailer and follow up with a telephone call to get an appointment. Rather than setting our sights on a narrowed list of prospects we felt confident we could convert to clients, we targeted everybody. (There's a reason that the saying is "Ready, aim, fire" and not "Fire, ready, aim.)

But today, building the descriptors of our target clients has gotten more sophisticated. If the more simplistic approach described above is representative of our dinosaur, the Tesla has many more bells and whistles.

Building out this extended target client description has evolved into an area of marketing focus unto itself: "persona development." With persona development, you create an idealized prospect that consists of multiple factors and goes far beyond the size, industry, and geography of their company. The persona is an embodiment of your ideal client (your "dream client," if you will); their description may also include items such as their buying behaviors, their interests and concerns, and their influencers. I've even seen personas given names, which really helped bring them to life.

Put simply, you need to know more about your targets than you did in the past. The old media channels and their outdated demographic descriptions that were relied upon in the past are dinosaurs today, ineffective, and more expensive than ever. But the more you customize your message and tactics to speak to the needs and interests of these personas, the more directly you speak to your audience.

Here's an example from my time at Plante Moran related to our plans to reach high-net-worth individuals. Our research showed that while these prospects received news from a number of sources, they were influenced about their choice of wealth management firms by their attorneys and peers more than any other source. As we put together a plan, we redirected money that had originally been planned for direct mail to clothing options for clients who attended an event we hosted. Why? We believed, if our clients wore a shirt with our logo, it might invite a question from a nonclient friend that could result in a new client. Our research indicated that this positioned us for success more than the direct mail piece we'd originally planned.

How to sketch your ideal target persona(s)

Building your target persona starts with many of the elements you've traditionally considered:

- How big is your dream client? Do their needs match your firm's capabilities?

- What other quantitative measures describe them?

- Staff size?

- Number of locations?

- Ownership structure (corporation, portfolio company, partnership)?

- Specialty areas?

- Number of years in business?

- Importance of foreign clients and suppliers?

- SIC code of core business?

- Who are their major suppliers?

- Who are their major customers?

Some of these categories may not apply in every situation, and there may be others you need to add. The goal is to arrive at a specific definition of your buyer and their role in their organization so your team can develop plans that are bespoke to them. Larger firms may have multiple personas who have similarities and differences to which they tailor specific strategies to get the most effective results.

In the digital world, additional information that's traditionally been outside of your target client development can help you engage with them in their online activity. Questions like:

- How are they influenced by others in their field?
- What's important to the decision-makers for business and outside of work?
- What's the unique intersection of this business and your service?
- How technologically savvy is the buyer?
- Will they engage in a lot of research about your service?
- How long is the buying cycle?
- Who is advertising to the buyer from a corporate and personal perspective?
- What other companies are trying to sell to them right now?
- Which associations are they likely to belong to?
- How do they use social media?
- Which news sources do they read?

Getting these answers, or making an educated guess, can give you a competitive advantage. For instance, you'll understand why trade shows carry so much weight in the buying decisions for healthcare, banking, higher education, K-12 schools, and govern-ment organizations and weight your marketing efforts toward them. You'll understand that technical papers may help your business gain attention for your expertise when CFOs and CIOs are influential in the buying process. On the flip side, you'll learn that, when you're targeting time-challenged C-suite decision makers, shorter and more impact-driven marketing content has a better chance of reaching them. The language used on your website and in your marketing materials will resonate more clearly when you've defined the personas of your target audience.

Other benefits to be gained by honing your understanding of the persona of your target audience include:

- Your plans will be sharper and more focused, and the results will be more measurable.

- Committing the definition of the persona to paper ensures that client servers and marketers agree. It allows your client servers the ability to educate the marketers and offer challenges if they don't believe the target client is properly characterized.

- Marketers can build the best integrated efforts to reach the audience. Your client servers may not agree with the tactics, and the team can sort through whether the disagreements are due to fact or the partner's personal preference. More times than not, they can agree on the best tactics to achieve the goals with everyone's professional opinions equally respected.

KNOWING WHO YOUR TARGET AUDIENCE IS NOT

I recall attending a two-day seminar where the topic was: "The business issues facing the commercial sectors." One staff used a Q&A segment to voice concern that the cab driver from the airport to the hotel didn't know that Plante Moran served internationally active clients. There was some general muttering of dissatisfaction and agreement until the head of the practice used it as a learning opportunity to remind the group that our marketing focus was very buyer specific (as opposed to general awareness), and it was no surprise that a taxi driver wouldn't know about the firm's international capabilities. This is a little bit of reverse engineering, but it shows why identifying the target buyer is so important for an organization. It helps to identify targets for both pursuits and marketing efforts.

Meet your prospects where they are to help them move forward

A while back, I helped plan a conference for Plante Moran's high-net-worth clients, and one session focused on how clients and families deal with memory loss issues. We had a great panel of legal and healthcare professionals. One of the best pieces of advice came from an estate planning attorney who offered that he worked frequently with clients with memory issues, and he began every meeting by summarizing the conversation covered in the last meeting. This accomplished two things: his clients weren't embarrassed about not remembering the previous conversation, and it set the table for what had already been agreed to by the client.

Similar advice is appropriate when initiating a "conversation" with a prospective client. Your research might reveal some general trends about potential business issues based on various factors you discover, but you don't know their individual situation until you hear from them. Take the time to find out where they are, and customize your approach based on what they say, rather than talking too much and risk losing a connection if they don't see themselves in the picture you paint.

Some of you may remember roadtrip maps called "TripTiks," which were the precursor to Google Maps for families who belonged to the AAA. In the days before vehicle navigation systems, you'd go to your local AAA office, and they'd give you paper maps with detailed driving instructions from your starting point to your destination. These "TripTiks" were customized to your trip.

A similar picture can be drawn for a prospect. Let's say you're hoping to sell ERP services to a manufacturing plant. The owner realizes the benefits of an ERP system but thinks they're too small for such an expensive investment. She doesn't realize that, in fact, they are big enough and, moreover, making that investment would result in a positive ROI. However, without first understanding her point of view and thought process, you'd have little chance to help because instead of talking about the benefits, you need to be talking about how ERP systems size up and down for different facilities. Until your prospects realize your service can help them today, they'll shut down for the essential part of the conversation because they don't think it applies.

Collaboration — it's more than just a 13-letter word

The most comprehensive use of target client descriptions will result when both practice staff and their marketing colleagues come together to create the plan to convert new prospects to clients.

Let's imagine we're targeting private equity fund managers. Our client servers know they're highly sophisticated people whose wealth and demanding schedules make it extremely difficult to attract their attention. A standard "run-of-the-mill" offer won't be enough. When the marketers and our client servers focus on the unique characteristics of these prospects, the chances for a creative solution that ensures the best chance for success are much improved.

For example, one creative option to reach the fund managers may be to help them meet the leaders of future portfolio companies. This might seem unorthodox, but creating an efficient way to put them in front of quality companies that may make good targets will certainly get their attention and give us a good shot at future work. This type of creative solution is possible when client servers and marketers understand the persona of the buyer and collaborate on creative solutions. Even if this idea isn't deployed, there's no arguing with the stream of logic that created it.

Summary

Identifying your target buyer has gotten a lot more complicated in the digital world. Today's targets are much more than the generic and impersonal statistics used to describe them just a few years ago. By creating personas, you can uncover details about your target that may give you a competitive advantage.

Look for new data points that will allow you to go beyond the expected trade publications to connect with your targets and really determine how to influence their buying decisions. Building the persona is a combination of facts, research, and educated guesses to create an ideal target that can be pursued by your digital strategy and your business developers.

GET OFF OF THAT DINOSAUR!

These questions will help you get out of The Stone Age and into The Digital Age. Ask yourself:

- Does your definition of your target buyer/persona give you new avenues to engage them in a business conversation? It will be hard to get a larger audience if you just use the same old avenues.

- Does the description of your target persona broaden what you know about their interests and how to engage them?

- Can you reduce the time from a prospect's first engagement with your organization to the first transaction by finding information to create more expediency?

See Tool 2 in the appendix for a short guide to develop a model persona of your ideal client.

The Whole Is Greater Than the Sum of Its Parts.

My father was into DIY (do it yourself) long before there was an acronym, and after every project there was always a mix of odds and ends that didn't get used. Dad stored these pieces away and filed them in his memory banks. Often, at a later time, these seemingly worthless pieces would get pulled from a bin or a box and would be just the thing needed to save the day for another project.

Our careers are like that: we pick up different kernels of knowledge which, initially, may seem of little value, but sometimes they're the valuable tidbits that can save the day for us later on.

I want to share with you a few such kernels that I picked up along the way. Many of them didn't seem particularly important in the moment but have become core to my foundation in successful marketing.

A marketing plan is the roadmap.

We'll discuss this in detail later on, but a marketing plan is the essential starting point for your strategy — and it should be updated annually. Then it should be communicated to appropriate stakeholders, adjusted as necessary, and all deliverables and time frames should be finalized.

One consistent theme throughout this journey is the weaknesses of single-tactic efforts and the importance of follow-up. In the past, relying solely on public relations might have been enough to make the phone ring, but the impact of any single media outlet has diminished as our audience's attention span has shortened (just like our own). Today, you need to deploy multiple integrated tactics to achieve a single goal. Your marketing plan is where all of those tactics come together.

Integrated marketing plan

An added benefit to a marketing plan is that it will avoid disrupting peak client service times. If you're like me, trying to fit 20 hours of client service work into a 12-hour day, there's rarely capacity to discuss marketing plan modifications or additions, let alone the planning itself.

The best marketing efforts are intentional, not happenstance.

A wise person once told me that, to be successful, we need to understand our clients and their needs and then tailor our services to those needs. Many organizations have failed when they tried instead to reengineer their clients to meet their needs.

We talked about defining your target buyer in Chapter 2; this is core to offering a tailored approach. The closer you get to the target, the more personalized the approach can be. Digital campaigns can make your pursuits more focused than what they've traditionally been, but as you talk to prospects in person, you need to make sure you understand them, before you get too far in the process. This requires intentionality.

Depending on where a new prospect is in the purchasing process will influence your strategy.

Ideally, conversations with prospects will begin early in the buying process, and often before the prospect has recognized a need for your service. That may not always be the case, and sometimes the need to build credibility is quicker than others.

Stay in front of your buyers by demonstrating your expertise and knowledge of their unique needs and perspectives.

This means leveraging technical skills, not your cocktail hour skills. You might offer a seminar series, newsletters, podcasts, and other targeted outreach that, when added to your personal interactions, gives you a great chance of winning when the time is right. Specialized content like case studies, online webinars, and other thought leadership are proven ways to build a favorable reputation for you and your firm. They create the foundation for a strong relationship where the prospect respects your technical expertise, has confidence in your approach, and trusts that you have their best interests in mind. Like and trust are important ingredients in the equation, but they're just table stakes. Technical competency must be front and center.

Use marketing and business (sales) development to move the needle.

While there's more on this topic in the next few chapters, the areas where sales and marketing professionals can best help you include:

- Creating an engaging and informative website that demonstrates a compelling case about your firm and the services you offer. The content should include discussion and examples that clearly explain the impact of your services. One caution: many marketing professionals write website content in a "neutral," informational way, like you would a piece of thought leadership. Your website is an advertisement for your firm — so write it like one. (You may need input from a business developer or a sales resource to get the convincing tone you want.)

- Avoiding proposals that are too wordy and/or don't succinctly answer the question, "Why are you the firm to hire?" (Note: Proposals are best written by proposal specialists versus marketing generalists.)

- Introducing digital tools that will help you attract more business and measure your effectiveness in doing so.

- Creating a thought leadership program that draws in and nurtures your prospects.

- Focusing on business development. These professionals can be counted on to:

  » Cold call prospects who haven't responded in other ways.

  » Project manage the sales process, so you can stay top of mind with prospects and avoid "silent periods" when partners have other client demands.

  » Moderate meetings with potential clients to make sure the prospect gets to voice their concerns before your team talks about how they can help.

  » Help to close the sales.

Anyone who wants to be a student of the selling process needs to first observe as a buyer. When you accept a meeting for a software vendor (they usually have the best-trained sales teams), watch how they approach the sales process. Typically, in the first meeting, they'll ask about your goals. They intentionally focus that meeting on you with very little information about them. The second meeting will start with a recap of what you told them in the first meeting and then bridge to them, their offering, and how they can help you achieve your goals.

I really enjoy observing this process and always learn so much. I also recommend this exercise to people who are new to selling; there's something to be said for watching how people who receive hundreds of hours of coaching and have lots of research on human behavior execute the process.

AS A BUYER, MY EXTENDED COURTSHIP WITH A TECH PROVIDER WAS WORTH IT IN THE END

I've found that we can learn a lot during the courting process about how a prospect fits on our "ideal client spectrum." When Plante Moran was selecting a company to help us with marketing technology solutions, I found that the "get-to-know-you" phase could extend for quite some time. During that time, we learned a lot about the firms under consideration, their approaches, and their insights. By the time we issued our RFP, we had our favorite — we already held them in an extremely high regard, and the RFP was just a formality and price check. In the process, we showed ourselves to be a good firm to work with and that we were looking for a partner rather than a "vendor." I'm sure it took longer than the firm that we selected wanted, but in the end, we had a great relationship.

Remember to enjoy the journey.

The last overarching piece of advice is to remember to enjoy the journey. When you're optimistic, intentional, and maintain a positive attitude, it's much easier to effect the change you want. I was fortunate to make great progress, but it took many attempts and lots of repetition. We know as leaders how hard it can be to make a change that people are anticipating, but changes that the team is hesitant about are even more challenging. I tried to laugh at myself and hold myself up as the "problem." That worked well for me — but something else might work better for you. In the end, however, change can't happen without positivity.

Summary

Back in the dinosaur days, annual marketing efforts were largely untargeted and disjointed; in today's Tesla world, you set your goal, invest in a plan, and value execution with generous process improvement along the way. The tools you use, like thought leadership, are calibrated to the prospects' needs, not your offerings. Intentional marketing efforts that are guided by a well-considered and integrated plan create the best opportunity for success — because they start with what's important to your prospects.

 GET OFF OF THAT DINOSAUR!

These tips will help you get out of The Stone Age and into The Digital Age:

- Create a marketing plan upfront that's customized to your specific goals, and exercise the discipline to check in monthly or quarterly.

- Ensure the prospect's issues are at the center of all pursuits.

- Take advantage of the opportunity to be a student of the sales process. When large sales pitches are made to you, see what you take away to make your next sale better.

See Tool 11 in appendix for a sample integrated marketing plan.

Section Two:
When You Need More Than a Jack of All Trades

If you're like most people, you probably consider yourself a jack of all trades. You've enjoyed success, and you trust your instincts, but the time comes in every growing organization when it goes from being dominated by a single personality to a team sport.

When this happens, the dynamics change, and the game rules need to fit the whole organization if they're to be successful. This is often where an organization's interest in professional marketing begins to grow. In the next few chapters, we'll explore how you can meet your firm's marketing needs, regardless of size.

4

Get Marketing and Sales Help: Where Do You Start?

You've decided to invest in marketing and sales to help your professional services firm grow. Congratulations! Making the decision to get help from marketing and/or sales professionals (business developers and salespeople are used interchangeably) isn't a choice to be made lightly, but be confident knowing that just as you've been trained in your area of specialty, they're similarly skilled in theirs.

Your decision will call for an investment of time and money: a dedicated budget, staff who are available to work with the marketing team you hire, and lastly, a commitment to the decision you've made. Before you make this leap, it's important to evaluate your options. The three most typical are:

- Hiring an outsourced marketing firm that can provide turnkey solutions.
- Hiring marketing and business development staff members on your payroll.
- A hybrid model that combines both.

Pros and cons of outsourcing

Before you hire any dedicated marketing resources, you may want to start with an outsourced model. It's a great way to see immediate results of your marketing investment.

While it may be pricey to outsource all of your marketing functions to a firm specializing in marketing, it may be a perfect way to get started, to expand functionality, and supplement peak growth needs. The benefit is that you only pay for what you use. Often, the assignments are project-based, which allows you to you tailor the service to your needs, manage the budget, and control the duration. For instance, let's say you have a small marketing team focused on proposals and newsletters and, after reading this book, you want to see how digital marketing can help your firm grow revenue. You could create a project and budget with an outside agency to do a trial for your firm. If it works, you can decide to hire someone to perform the duties full time, or you can continue to outsource.

However, when you outsource, you still need to be involved. It's like buying a new suit: you can't skip the fittings and expect to receive one that's perfectly tailored. To get the marketing result you want, you still need to spend some time on guidance. While some professional service firms don't consider this option sustainable long term, most firms use outside consultants in an ongoing capacity on a project basis.

Building a team from scratch

At some point, you'll face the proverbial "make vs. buy" decision when you can bring the function in-house cheaper than paying an external consultant. When you decide to hire your own team, you should plan to add at least two people to start: a more experienced person and a more junior person. In my experience, it's rare that a single qualified person will be adept at both strategic tasks and detailed tasks. If one person says they like to do it all, proceed cautiously. Sometimes people will tell you whatever you want to hear, hoping they can convince you to change your mind when they start. Typically, if you don't change your mind, they don't stay around for more than a year.

Unlike outsourcing, building a team from the ground up takes time. You need to decide what you want to accomplish from your marketing efforts, define the skills you need, hire the people, and onboard them to your firm. Your new additions will need to thoroughly understand your unique differentiators, target clients, service lines, segments served, and distribution channels to be successful. They'll also be concerned about their own career path, so you'll need to be able to paint a picture of what that might look like if they can help you grow the firm.

With a small team, it may be hard to get all of the expertise you need to accomplish your goals, so you'll likely still need to supplement your internal team with outside skills — at least until the new team gets ramped up. However, this transition time can also serve as a training opportunity for your internal resources because they can learn important skills from the consultants. After your team learns these skills, you can transfer tasks.

Your reward for building your in-house team? You own and control the proprietary knowledge from your efforts, and it will stay inside your firm.

To enjoy the most success, it's important to establish your growth goals upfront. This way, you can establish how you'll measure success, define the investments you're willing to make, and even project what the marketing team might look like five years down the road. This will be different for a $1,000,000 organization versus a $20,000,000 organization, but with your goals and size in mind, a little reverse engineering can often be helpful to build a five-year staffing plan. With this long-term view as a basis, you can efficiently focus on the talent and resources to meet your goals.

Beware, though, that as you add marketing resources, they can easily be overwhelmed. In most organizations, demands from client servers easily outstrip the capacity of marketing teams. To keep the team focused to meet the goals you've established and keep the job satisfaction for your marketers high, you'll need to serve as a gatekeeper to make sure the most important tasks get done and less important tasks don't jam up the wheels of progress. If there are requests that you deprioritize, you'll need to be the one to deny the request. This exercise will assure that top priorities are met and may also open your eyes to demands for additional resources.

The number-one reason for job dissatisfaction by professional service marketers is the overwhelming frustration of never being able to satisfy the demands placed before them. You'll need to help set priorities — and communicate those priority to your partners. If their priorities don't align with yours, they'll need to authorize more marketing team members. This will allow you to keep the good staff you've hired.

GIVE CREDIT WHERE CREDIT IS DUE

I've seen anxious partners rely heavily on marketers while courting a client and developing a proposal. No mistake, this is a great use of marketing talent. But, when firm leaders learned about the opportunity, marketing's help was only mentioned as ancillary. The partners claimed to do most of the work themselves.

The problem this example creates is that firm leaders don't know that marketing had 60 hours invested in the new client pursuit. If that happens 10 times in a year, which is realistic, there's a quarter of the year left unaccounted for, and leaders assume marketing was working on the other goals assigned. If you want to invest in the growth for your firm, marketing support is a great investment. Managed appropriately, you can have your eyes wide open and know when you can justify increasing your spend.

The hybrid model — the best of both worlds

Much like "Goldilocks and The Three Bears," professional service firms often find focusing solely on outsourcing or in-house staff to be uncomfortable — but a hybrid approach may be "just right."

The hybrid marketing model allows you to have the best of both worlds. Add capacity and expertise, but only pay for what you need and no more.

We used the hybrid model for some highly specialized writing projects, like tax. It didn't justify a full-time staff, so we just paid for what we used. It was a great way to augment the team's capabilities, and contract resources were also useful to fill holes created by people who took family medical leave.

Champagne taste on a beer budget

Before you start hiring, try and project what a mature marketing team organization chart might look like in, say, five years. Think about what you want the marketing function to deliver to your organization and how you'll measure and evaluate the goals, whether new clients, more development dollars, more members, higher average client size, etc. Whatever it is, quantify it and then build the team that can deliver.

Then consider what percentage of revenue you're willing to invest in growth to estimate a budget. You can find statistics in various fields on what others are spending on marketing as a data point. In professional services, I've seen a large range of 0.5 –10%. Armed with these data points, create an organization chart.

Once I have my future state in mind, I always find it easier to work backward to determine my starting point. This will make each addition consistent with your long-term vision, create a strategy where your efforts will build on one another, and get the most important tasks done first.

Defining your marketing ROI

An important element in building your resource and establishing your budget is to define your expected ROI (return on investment) on your marketing spend. Computing your marketing ROI is relatively straightforward. For instance, if your firm has been growing organically at 3%

per year without any marketing support, how much more growth will you need to justify a marketing spend? Things you might consider:

- What percentage increase in revenue over the status quo would justify the additional expense?

- What ROI do you expect from the dollars you spend on marketing? If you spend $100, do you expect it will help generate an incremental $1,000?

- If marketing helps you attract new clients, how much revenue will you get over the lifetime of those new clients? And consider more than just the initial investment. Even if the investment to get a client equals the revenue billed in year one, remember that there's potential to serve them indefinitely — as long as you've built a solid relationship.

With these types of questions in mind, you can make an intentional decision that will be transparent, objective, and measurable. Your criteria should also clarify when the measurement period will begin, the allotted time to ramp up to speed, and the first measurement point.

One caveat. The buying cycle for most professional service firm clients is 3–10 years. If you're hiring a marketing director or CMO, you'll need to give that person time to get oriented and find resources (staff or consultants) to execute their plans. If you set quarterly activity goals, you can measure the ramp-up to your ultimate goals. Some activities you might measure are first appointments with new prospects, requests for proposal, website inquiries, and new subscribers to thought leadership.

Not allowing enough lead-time to reach the ultimate goal is a common issue and can lead to a revolving door of marketing talent. On the other hand, allowing too much time is like throwing money out of the window. There's probably no absolute answer, but the insights that result from the discussions around benchmarks certainly inform your evaluation.

NOT-SO-COMMON SENSE TIPS TO KEEP IN MIND

1. Good marketing and sales professionals are good business people. I can introduce you to many. We present logical, fact-based business decisions. We can explain how we arrived at our assumptions and what ROI we expect. All of our activities impact growth — because there isn't time for the "nice-to-haves." The more we work together, the more you trust us. We're as focused on the growth goal as you are. Creativity is not crazy!

2. An administrative assistant who has a knack for ordering nice promo items that everyone likes is still primarily an administrative assistant who has a flair for promo items. Moving them to marketing is not a legitimate start to your marketing spend.

3. Watch out for the advice from a partner who took marketing or sales classes more than 10 years ago and who claims to have an expertise. They may be very good at business development, but that doesn't equate to leading the marketing function for your firm.

4. You get what you pay for, and if you aren't paying your marketing resource more than your interns, you probably aren't getting much. Be wary of people who are making below the going wage.

5. A member of your client service team who doesn't have the right skill set to finish the journey to partner and has never been particularly good at bringing in new business will not miraculously become a good salesperson/business developer if you change their focus.

Firms who are going through this process for the first time should find a marketing professional who can help them identify goals and set measurements. A consultant with this experience will help you establish the fundamentals, put together a six-month program, write job descriptions, and help with interviewing. This process can give you a detailed plan before you begin hiring and can jumpstart your efforts.

Summary

There are multiple ways to add marketing and business development skills to any size organization, but it begins with understanding what you want to accomplish. This informs how you best assign resources to meet your short- and long-term goals. Many organizations benefit from setting a five-year goal and organization design and then working backwards to what makes the most sense today. This can seem overwhelming when you aren't comfortable with marketing. Beginning with the help of a professional will establish a solid foundation for years to come.

GET OFF OF THAT DINOSAUR!

These tips will help you get out of The Stone Age and into The Digital Age:

- Establish incremental revenue goals that you want marketing and sales resources to help achieve.

- When considering starting a marketing team, consider your goals and the skills necessary to accomplish them before you write a job description.

- Whether you're starting a marketing team from scratch or growing your team, create a flexible plan that allows you to prove success before you make a final purchase decision.

- Determine your options for hiring a sales professional, and get help to establish a compensation plan to attract and retain professionals.

- Put a score card together that tracks key metrics of your marketing leadership in a transparent and objective way.

5

Hiring Your Sales and Marketing Leaders.

You've decided to hire a marketing and sales leader, recruiting has found a candidate, and the interview goes well. The candidate has spoken earnestly about their experience and offered up impressive ideas sprinkled with marketing catchphrases. Their eye contact and smile reassures you that, yes, you really like them. But how do you differentiate the marketing gibberish from knowledge? And how do you separate the non-answers from the truth nuggets that demonstrate real expertise?

When it comes to hiring, most professional service firms are skilled at finding the right candidates who will excel at serving their clients. Law firms know how to hire lawyers. Accounting firms are good at hiring CPAs. Consulting firms know what's in the DNA for a good consultant.

Unfortunately, these reliable methods may not work when professional service firms are hiring marketing and sales professionals, especially when those who are tasked with hiring marketing leadership aren't marketing or sales professionals themselves.

Why do so many searches fail? It begins with a flawed recruiting process that's compounded by ineffective onboarding and supervision. At about two years, most firms call foul when the candidate has failed to meet expectations, and the process starts again. We can all agree that there's room for improvement.

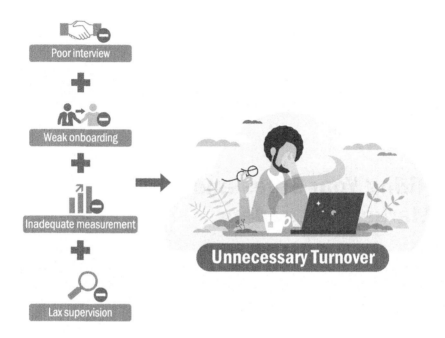

We all make hiring mistakes occasionally, but even then, if there's a good orientation and performance management plan that's transparent and consistently followed, it won't take two years to identify a bad hire. Establishing clear objectives and measurements in the first week, which are reviewed quarterly, will set a clear tone of accountability.

Generally, most firm leaders delegate a cursory orientation and then leave it to the new hire to "do what they do." Since many firm leaders dread the process so much and are uncomfortable with sales and marketing, they're overly generous with new hires about measurement criteria. This works to the detriment of the candidate and the firm, because issues that can be easily addressed are usually deferred until they become too big to solve.

It doesn't have to be that hard! If you get help from a marketing professional, you can avoid many of the most common pitfalls. Here are the steps to follow for a successful search:

- Identify goals that the successful candidate will achieve to help the firm with its growth targets.

- Develop a clear job description that includes the experience needed to achieve your goals.

- Develop 3-4 screener questions that HR can use as part of the phone screen. Make them specific to the job.

- Develop a brief "case study" for candidates to complete before their in-person interview. (Answers may not be perfect, but it gives you good insight into their marketing toolbox, critical thinking skills, and knowledge of your profession.)

- Develop a standard set of interview questions that each interviewer will use.

- Share the goals with the candidates and seek feedback.

- Hire a marketer professional with equal or greater skills of the position you're hiring for to interview on your behalf.

Throughout the interview, pay attention to the candidate's proficiency in digital marketing technology and writing skills.

I hate to say this about my own tribe, but after hiring hundreds of marketing and sales individuals, I've found that oftentimes they're better at selling themselves than they would ever be at delivering the help our firms need. Add to that the skills gap that occurs when professionals don't stay current in their own field, and it's no wonder that the challenge of hiring a good resource is difficult.

Today, we can't just say all marketers are created equal. Marketing has totally changed in the last 10 years: most college marketing classes are out of date for anyone who graduated more than five years ago because they didn't have so many of the digital tools and skills that are now core skills. If a marketer hasn't kept up with the latest techniques, you'll either need to send them to training or go without the expertise, which may put you at a competitive disadvantage. You have one chance to do this well. You need to pay attention to any misgivings you have about a candidate, no matter how much you like them or how well they're recommended.

LISTEN TO YOUR GUT

One time I was desperately in need of a marketing consultant, and I let my guard down. We had a well-groomed candidate whose spouse owned a business and worked in a related field. We had mutual friends, and they came with a good endorsement from a trainer we used. The candidate was very polished and knew the answers we wanted to hear. Others in the hiring process had concerns, but with our pressing need, I convinced the team that we could take a risk. "How bad could it be," I thought.

Almost on day one, I realized I'd made a mistake. Despite the candidate claiming they'd written a white paper on a very hot topic, we found their writing skills were horrible. We also found that their endorsements were more related to friendships and loyalty rather than skill. That was the last time I let my feelings get the better of me, and we instituted a required writing test for all future candidates.

As an aside, we also found that Excel skills are a good indicator of a person's ability to effectively use our CRM and made that test a requirement at the same time. In our digital age, marketers need to be able to use the tools, not just talk about them effectively.

Be clear about your goals

As you begin the hiring process for your next CMO or CBDO (chief business development officer), articulating your goals for the position is crucial and will inform all of the other steps. When you're identifying goals, you should also include quantifiable metrics other than revenue growth, openly discuss these goals during the interview, and get the candidate's input on the best ways to accomplish them. By sharing your goals in the interview, their answers will provide insight into how well they match your vision.

So how should you evaluate your new CMO? "Increasing sales" likely comes to mind, but your partners play such a large role in closing a sale that you can't hold marketing solely responsible. You should also identify quantifiable goals that are led by marketing initiatives and, if done well, will result in more sales leads.

In future chapters we'll discuss several marketing strategies that could be the basis for these quantifiable goals. Meanwhile, below are several goals that you could consider right away:

- Leads or inquiries/RFPs sent to the website (Can they increase inquiries by 10% over the 12 months before they started?)
- New audience members attending webinars or new subscribers to newsletters
- Open rates on emails
- Visitors to your website
- Increase in proposal win rates

These measures work well because they're both measurable and central to helping grow your business.

Once you've evaluated and compared all the inputs from interview questions, the candidate's response to the case studies, and their cultural fit, you're ready to make your choice. Hopefully, all the interviewers will meet to discuss the strengths and weaknesses of each candidate. With this level of involvement, you can have confidence that you're executing a fact-based decision.

Onboarding

Congratulations, your candidate is on the job. Now it's time to lay the groundwork for their success. In the first week, go back through the data you captured in the interview process with your new hire. (You can also use the data points collected in the interview to establish the initial goals.) This would be a great time to share what the interview committee viewed as the new hire's strengths and opportunities. If there were areas of concern raised by the committee, get them out in the open right away. Creating a transparent plan to discuss the improvement areas periodically will help you avoid any surprises and perhaps provide the opportunity to offer support before anything becomes insurmountable. It would be a shame to have a known weakness go unattended and result in failure.

As the onboarding begins, you might consider the following actions:

- Prioritize your goals. You can't get everything done at once, but if you prioritize, your new hire will know where to start.

- Ask the candidate to put together a two-year plan to ramp up strategies to meet your goals.

- Set quarterly measurements to assess progress.

Summary

You can lead a successful recruiting effort for your next CMO if you follow a rigorous process and get the help you need to evaluate the candidate — internally from the interview team and/or externally from an experienced marketer. By creating a detailed onboarding program, establishing measurable goals, and addressing any questions that came up during the interview process, you can leverage lessons learned and increase the opportunity for success.

 GET OFF OF THAT DINOSAUR!

These tips will help you get out of The Stone Age and into The Digital Age:

- Get help from a marketing professional who will serve as your outside coach. Even if you have a great recruiting team, they don't hire this position often. A technical coach and screener can help you design the job description, articulate goals, and develop your case study and screener questions.

- When working with your recruiter and marketing professional, set aside a day in advance for the in-person interviews. This should be 60–90 days out. Setting aside this time will create a call to action versus HR letting you know when they have someone for you to meet. Preferably your recruiter and marketing professional will have met the candidates beforehand and eliminated people who didn't fit well.

- For the recruiting process, set up a weekly scorecard that includes:
  - » Number of applicants
  - » Number of telephone screens
  - » Number of in-person interviews conducted (if considering an out-of-town candidate, spend the money to fly the person in to meet with the recruiting team on a day different than when you're supposed to meet with the candidate)
- Understand your compensation range upfront. Stay away from people who are below and above the range.
- Be cautious about hiring someone who's been an independent consultant to come "in house" as your marketing leader. It can be difficult for someone who's used to working with several clients to be able to settle in to a one-client situation. It's not impossible, but it's worthy of close communication to make sure your new hire continues to feel positive about their decision.

Below is a list of additional content in the appendix as it relates to hiring marketing/sales help:

- Tool 3 in the appendix: Process to Create a Marketing Job Description Tailored to Your Firm
- Tool 4 in the appendix: Sample CMO Job Description
- Tool 5 in the appendix: Sample Marketing Scientist Job Description
- Tool 6 in the appendix: Outline of a Successful Interview Process
- Tool 7 in the appendix: Potential Interview Questions for Marketing Leaders and Staff
- Tool 8 in the appendix: Case Studies for Marketing Candidates to Demonstrate Skills

6

Business Developer Compensation and Management.

In a perfect world, every partner in a professional service organization would be responsible for growing the firm and would be eager to do so. There would be no resentment about having to sell, no anxiety about selling skills, and no complaints that serving clients takes 120% of a partner's time so there's no time to spare. In this ideal world, there'd be no need for business developers.

But reality is tough medicine, and many professional service firms that are serious about growth have changed their view and decided to hire a business developer. These sales professionals work alongside the partners and together create a united force that identifies, grooms, and wins new business. It's a team effort; I've never seen a model where anyone is working solo and delivering signed engagement letters without the help of others.

How to hire, compensate, and manage business developers is one of the least written about and most misunderstood areas in professional service firms. This chapter is intended to add more clarity on how to structure compensation plans, how to peg total compensation, how to create a model that ramps up to full commission and, most importantly, how to hire and manage a new business development role.

What, exactly, is a business developer?

Business developers are not synonymous with marketers, but they are a critical element of the marketing ecosystem. While most partners in a wealth management, management consulting, legal, or accounting firm will have new business (business development) goals and client service goals, when I refer to business developers, I'm talking about people whose sole focus is sales — people who help convert targets to clients through personalized efforts.

Business developers will cold call prospects, meet with prospects to hear their issues and show how the firm can help them, form client pursuit teams, work on proposal efforts, and often speak as the voice of the prospect to marketing. At Plante Moran, we didn't have business developers who met alone with prospects but they worked as part of a pursuit team, often as meeting planners and moderators.

You don't know what you don't know

Why are we talking about compensation and management? Most firms have only a few business developers, and their HR resources may have little insight into how they should be paid or ways to structure sales compensation plans. Is it the size of the engagement? The lifetime value of a new client to your firm? There's scant information about what goes into a compensation model for professional service firms, and specific survey data can be hard to find. I found most accurate information is shared by word of mouth in individual conversations or blind surveys at conferences. Most of the published data is hard to interpret and use.

Another factor to consider is the way that new digital marketing tools have expanded the business case for business developers. These new tools make it possible for your marketing team to automate sales attraction techniques that previously were completed through personal interaction. As these tools pull qualified leads through the sales process, they can identify the point when a personal interaction might accelerate the process. By using a business developer at this stage, you can avoid unnecessary use of partner time until it's efficient for them to be introduced to the prospect and join the process.

Hiring and compensating a business developer

Between opening doors with new prospects, complementing your digital efforts, and project managing through the sale process, business developers may be more important to growing a firm than ever. While these contributions add value, the greatest weight should be placed on their ability to get that first appointment with a new prospect. How do you attract a business developer with this skill, and where do you find them?

In an earlier chapter, we talked about the need to understand the demographics of clients and prospects: that data is essential when hiring a business developer. Obviously, the more experience and connections a business developer has with decision-makers in your target markets, the faster they'll bring in new business. Their years of experience and well-developed network will inform their salary expectations, so don't make the mistake of driving a bargain basement salary: again, you get what you pay for today.

I've worked with hundreds of salespeople and business developers in my life, and for a long time I wasn't focused on hiring the "best of the best." I looked for good, solid professionals who I thought could grow to understand our business and network. I was more focused on the best for what I wanted to pay. While I've watched some people really blossom, it takes a while, and sadly, the wait often was more expensive than I wanted to admit.

So my philosophy changed. Today I think you should hire the most experienced person you can afford. I view it like planting a privacy hedge around your patio. You can plant one-foot seedlings and wait for them to grow. Or you can invest more upfront and plant eight-foot mature trees. You'll get instant privacy with the eight-foot trees and, if you're like me, that's worth paying for since I'm not getting any younger.

But how do you know what you can afford to pay? The deeper question is the subset of the broader question: what should you pay? As a rule, the business developer you hire should be held accountable to bring in at least four-to-six times their compensation in new revenue by their third year of employment. If they're within 80%, you have someone to work with, but below that, you must seriously consider their long-term potential to meet your needs. It probably isn't economical to have someone who's not generating that level of business. You shouldn't pay your business developer more than they help generate in sales, although many do and justify it by saying that these professionals have other value or that they're being trained in sales techniques. Don't accept this excuse. If you need a sales trainer, hire one; it'll probably be cheaper than a business developer.

All this is to say, hire the best salesperson you can afford. I define "best" by a proven track record of selling more than $1 million of new business a year and having a high number of contacts who you would consider decision-makers for purchasing your services. Successful executive recruiters are often considered to be great business developer candidates because they have a close network of decision-makers. Who doesn't love the person who helped you get the job you love? But be prepared to spend a lot. This is where some people's stomachs sour, but I argue that if you follow the four-to-six times comp rule in setting your sales quota, your firm will be a winner in the end. Even with a higher salary.

Good salespeople are goal-driven and are used to tough love. As we discussed in Chapter 4, the worst thing you can do (and what most people do) is hire them and forget about them. Instead, I recommend a robust and frequent touch-base routine.

- Meet with them biweekly for 30–60 minutes.
- Give them a chance to showcase what went well — and talk about what they need to be successful.

- Set predefined activity levels, and ensure they meet or exceed them. For instance, you might require they set four appointments per week and send an email to five connections to tell them they changed employers. (I would start with smaller weekly goals while they learn your firm and accelerate to a number you feel confident will set them on a trajectory to meet their two-to-three-year goal).

- Understand and talk about the contacts they're making. Most of their contacts won't be ready to make a buying decision today, but if it takes 18 months for them to come around, the more seeds of opportunity are being sowed for the future. If the seeds aren't planted, the sales get pushed out. It's difficult to overcome the natural curve of the sales process, so your business developer must get to work immediately. This is where asking their contacts to subscribe to your thought leadership and friending them on LinkedIn can be good first steps.

When you onboard a new business developer, it's important to take the time to help them get grounded in your organization.

- Orient them to the services you offer and how those services benefit your clients.

- Introduce the profile of your ideal client so they're hunting for the best prospects for the firm.

- Help them create a list of the top 20 decision-makers they know and how your services would apply.

- Help them create an introduction to your firm.

- Make sure that, when they get an appointment, you have a partner available to go with them. (Partners shouldn't have challenges with this.)

- Have each of your partners include them in at least one of their active pursuits.

- Rinse and repeat. After 90 days, go back through the list. With so much new material, it's hard to retain a large percentage with only one exposure.

Structuring compensation

Your model will likely consist of a salary component and a commission component. The best salespeople will be accustomed to this model. For professional services, you'll be looking at a high salary and a smaller commission.

You have lots of flexibility in structuring the commission. Most professional service firms allow the business developer to benefit from revenue from the client over two or three years on a declining basis. For instance, it might be 10% year-one revenue, 5% year-two and 2% year-three. You can tailor a plan that's right for your firm.

I also recommend that commission is only paid if the quarterly revenue target is hit. For instance, if a salesperson has an annual quota of $1 million, then their quarterly target is $250,000. No commission is paid unless they hit $250,000. I would have a year-to-date true-up each quarter, so if the salesperson catches up, there won't be a financial penalty. This is an incentive to hit the number and some financial protection for your firm if they're under-performing.

Finally, since salespeople generally make a salary and commission, and presumably they may not get to their full commission level for two years or more, you should construct a "bridge plan" based on a declining payment that allows your new salesperson the opportunity to build their new business without a steep financial penalty. If you're trying to hire the best, don't expect that they'll volunteer for a cut in pay for the honor of working at your firm despite their hopes for long-term potential. You should tie these supplemental payments to activities designed to fill the funnel and generate new business with a minimum level of activities required to get the payment that quarter — for instance, seven first appointments, five networking events, and 12 LinkedIn posts.

Other ways to get business development help without hiring expensive talent

What do you do if your business model won't allow for the expense of a proven sales professional? As we discussed, you could follow my first philosophy and hire a person at a low base and commission. Let them learn on the job. As their expertise increases, you may need to bump their salary to retain them, but you'll have proven value at that point. One of my friends started out this way and, after he proved his worth, he was made a partner in the firm. It probably wasn't part of the original thought, but it was a good business decision.

You could also partner with an outside firm that's paid based on activity or success. I worked with an amazing telemarketing firm that's truly a business partner. I would give them names of organizations that we wanted to penetrate, and they'd work to get us appointments. The cost was economical and the results good. Telemarketing firms aren't all created equal, but if you can find a good one, they can be a great partner in your efforts.

Lastly, you could also hire an independent representative — a professional who represents high-quality firms in different areas and has a good reputation. You can specify the targets you are looking to attract and get leads when they're uncovered.

Don't forget your safety net

When you're building a compensation structure, you should always have a "windfall provision" as a safety net. This is to avoid paying an exorbitant commission when the commission may not be commensurate with the effort.

For instance, let's say that the value of a new piece of business goes from $10,000 to $1,000,000. Your business developer is part of a team working on a new case and, through a merger, the firm where you've proposed acquires a much larger organization. They hire your firm, but you don't feel that the commission rate should be applied to the full revised value of the new deal amount. A windfall provision gives you the ability to adjust a commission payout. You may choose to pay more than what would originally be earned but cap the whole payout at a fixed amount. This is your protection, and it's usually only used in extreme circumstances. Of course, it must be included in the compensation agreement.

Managing the business developer

When it comes to managing a business developer to get the optimum performance, it's important to realize that the best business developers crave interaction and attention. I've seen many organizations adopt a "hands-off" approach, which is the opposite of what works best. They want to be held accountable, and they want to talk about their successes. While we never want to "over manage," anyone, business developers benefit from a more hands-on approach. I recommend weekly or biweekly half-hour meetings to monitor activities, assist with obstacles and, most importantly, hear about successes. Don't make the mistake of just telling them to just let you know if they need anything. Good business developers don't work like that. On the other hand, poorly performing business developers love it. It means less scrutiny and a longer timeline before someone figures out they're not delivering.

A couple of other key points about business developers that I want to touch on relates to who to hire and how they handle leads that come into the website.

A nagging question that many have about their business developer is, "How do you know that they're actually initiating new business and not simply just living off the website-generated leads?" The process in many firms is to give website leads to client servers (practice staff) and relegate the business developers as "hunters." They believe that a website lead is a "hot" lead, and there isn't much work involved in closing. While I think it's easy to draw this conclusion — IT'S NOT TRUE.

Despite their best intentions, practice staff easily get distracted when a new business opportunity doesn't close in one or two meetings, (which they don't at least 95% of the time). While they understand it can take longer, reality takes over, and client responsibilities cause them to put off the required follow-up tasks. This reality alone is a major justification for business developers and the incremental skills they bring with their ability to "project manage" pursuits.

For many, paying a business developer for website leads can be a sore spot, but I've never seen a website lead go to close in one or two meetings. And these opportunities can easily be lost because of an exhausting game of telephone tag, other demands on the seller's schedule, prolonged buyer decisions, and the lack of seller's confidence to get the buyer's commitment. I can't emphasize enough how important full-time business developers are to the process if you're serious about firm growth.

Benchmarks bring transparency to business development

Just as your CMO needs time to build resources and orient themselves to your firm, a business developer will need time to develop a "funnel" to meet your sales expectations. In my experience, a decent business development professional should deliver at least four times their total compensation in sales — but this isn't a fair measurement until 24–36 months (if we're counting cash collected, which is a typical way for professional service firms to count and pay commissions). So how do you know that you're not being taken advantage of in the meantime?

Good question. One year isn't enough time for leads to progress all the way to signed deals and payment in a quantity that's sufficient to fully support your hiring decision. Just as you establish performance criteria results for your CMO, you can measure activities that will indicate whether your business developer is on the right track. Some examples might include:

- Number of first appointments generated by the salesperson (i.e., in addition to leads from our website)
- Number of networking events attended
- Increase in LinkedIn network
- Number of network posts
- Number of people who attend hosted events

I've said that we shouldn't expect full quota until 24–36 months, but we should start to assign quota goals in the interim. In the model we followed at my former firm, we paid commission quarterly, and we'd start a partial commission in the 9–12-month period. In some cases, we might offer a commission subsidy until the person was fully ramped up in their sales.

Summary

You've heard the saying, "The only thing worse than no deal is a bad deal." There's a science to business developers' compensation, and it's worth the effort to seek advice outside your firm, if needed, to get it right. Like connecting with your prospects to have the most success, you need to put yourselves in the shoes of your business developers and create a plan that works for both of you.

GET OFF OF THAT DINOSAUR!

These tips will help you get out of The Stone Age and into The Digital Age:

- Track activities, sales, and commissions quarterly. Set up a specific meeting to discuss lessons learned and what else needs to happen to increase new revenue.

- Be open to ideas to help the business developer get more appointments. Offer to host a dinner for their best prospects or rent a suite at a sporting event or concert.

- Don't put a cap on commissions; the more they sell the better. The more they sell, the lower the overall commission percentage you're paying.

- Make sure any commission has a "windfall" provision.

See Tool 9 in the appendix for a meeting agenda of a business developer.

See Tool 10 in the appendix for a sample table of how to develop business developer's compensation.

Section Three:
Digital Transformation

When you think "digital transformation," you likely think "new technology." And that's part of it. But it's also updating traditional marketing practices with new strategies and processes.

Remember the iceberg from the introduction to this book? It's a fitting analogy here. Digital tools can best be represented by the portion of an iceberg that's below the water line, powerful but hidden from view. To get the full value from these tools, it's important to adopt new strategies — things like "content gating" where you exchange insights for readers' email addresses. And speaking of content, be prepared to change how you construct it — radically. Gone are the days of revealing your conclusion at the end of the fifth paragraph. Today, the big reveal may be the first thing you share.

In this section, we'll go through many of the elements you must consider to leverage these new tools and capture the attention of an audience with changing preferences.

7

The Tools of This New Trade.

Remember when buying a house was a complex and time-intensive process that filled many of us with dread? Back then you needed a trusted realtor to help you find the perfect home in the ideal neighborhood. A well-informed realtor could steer you through numerous real estate landmines: They knew what was on the market, the pros and cons of each neighborhood, and they wouldn't let you overpay. More times than not, they also helped you find your mortgage broker.

Then came the mortgage application process: hours of digging through old files to find tax returns and other important papers, filling out multiple forms by hand, and the excruciating wait for the final determination. Home buyers today still have tough decisions to make, but websites like realtor.com and software tools from mortgage lenders simplify the search and application process. It's possible to find a home and be approved for a mortgage all in an afternoon from the comfort of your living room (though I wouldn't recommend it!).

Just as technology has revolutionized the home-buying process, digital tools are revolutionizing professional services marketing.

Marketing software is more powerful and far-reaching than all your traditional marketing tactics on steroids — because it can independently cultivate prospective clients without your direct involvement. These technologies unleash new capabilities and unprecedented performance measurements that are immediately available in a transparent manner. Email wasn't opened by any recipients? You'll know immediately. Thought leadership article goes viral? You'll know immediately.

Despite these advances, there are still "old guard" rainmakers who are convinced that professional services is a "relationship business" and that investing in new, digital tools is a waste of money. (There may be a few realtors saying that too, but they're retiring at a fast rate.) This isn't to say that your firm's successful rainmakers have lost their touch or are no longer effective. Relationships still matter, and if their contacts don't retire, then you can continue to count on their ability to drive new business. The question is: how long can you ride that wave?

The number of people who buy the "old-school way" decreases every day, and there's too much at stake for you to ignore what's happening in the digital landscape and the competitive advantages it offers. While professional services, wealth management, and not-for-profit development marketing lag consumer marketing, digital marketing tools are being embraced by many of your competitors. Some knowledgeable sources have gone as far as to say that deferring these digital investments may be another reason organizations will be forced into mergers.

The importance of a digital roadmap

It's true that professional service firms, wealth management firms, and not-for-profits are investing in digital tools, but my impression is their purchases are more opportunistic than systematic or holistic. The tendency is to buy what's hot or what your peers are buying, creating digital islands that aren't linked to other enabling technologies. Acquiring software in this random pattern won't deliver the full benefit you require. You need to create a blueprint of your end-to-end architecture of the necessary tools.

The fact that the digital landscape is constantly changing certainly adds a challenge to creating your vision. At times it might be described as nailing spaghetti to the wall. Add your vulnerability to a good sales pitch or competitor adoption and it's easy to be led astray. So where do you start?

By arming yourself with a broad understanding of what's possible, you'll then be in a better position to make rational decisions and lay out a roadmap of the tools necessary to move from the capabilities you have today to the tools necessary to realize your vision. This is your best chance to make smart investment decisions that reflect the ROI your firm expects.

In my personal journey, I realized that even with the best under-standing, sometimes I just had to learn the hard way because technological advances are fluid and some ambiguity is expected. Sometimes you just need to "ride the wave." I can recall frustration when selecting an email platform, because each software offered different features — and they were always changing. Even harder, the changes were going in different directions and sometimes included promised features that never became functional. Until we created a decision model, which helped us navigate the choices by clarifying what our critical items were, we had a hard time making a unified decision on our technology investment.

Your digital ecosystem

Good client service skills will never go out of style, and neither will sales basics. However, the right digital marketing tools can simplify the prospecting process for busy professionals.

We already know that technology is improving and automating other parts of your business. Imagine how litigation firms are using artificial intelligence (AI) for document review — without it, they'd risk obsolescence. AI is working in a similar way to generate more leads based on your firm's digital prospect definition. Instead of hours following bad prospects, some business development hours can be redirected to chargeable work because of efficiency and time savings. Not taking advantage of these tools when they're deployed by your competitors will drive up comparative new client acquisition costs.

The main components in a digital ecosystem are:

- Website
- Content
- Subscriptions
- Contact information
- Lead generation and nurturing tools
- Human capital (digital scientist or analyst)

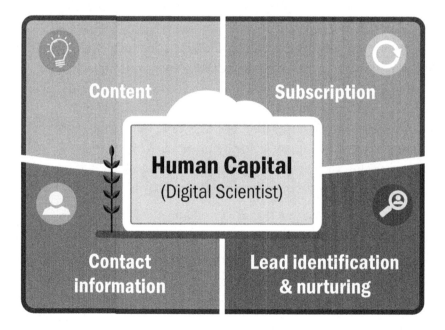

These elements are interdependent, and each of them makes a unique contribution to a digital ecosystem that will support your firm's growth plans. You may not acquire all of the tools needed to support your digital ecosystem in one fell swoop, but they all should figure into an overall digital roadmap, just like a new golf club complements or replaces something already in your bag.

But wait, there's more.

The elements in a digital marketing ecosystem rely on good, underlying software, people, and imagination. These are often unchartered waters. Some basic elements required are:

- Content engine (CMS or content management system)
- Publishing software (email platform, webinar, social, video, and podcast)
- Connected LinkedIn profiles
- Digital data warehouse (defined below)
- Artificial intelligence (AI) focused on identifying heightened interest by the buyer

The driving idea is to create compelling information that your prospects find useful and to expand your audiences to create even more prospects. Successfully doing this is the key to using digital tools as part of your business development efforts.

The following overview will help you better understand each of these elements so that you can have a knowledgeable conversation with your CMO about how digital marketing will be implemented at your firm.

Your website — the "front door" to your firm

Done well, your website is one of your biggest selling tools. It functions like a front door to your business. It presents your firm in a logical manner, describes your services in a compelling way, and offers content that supports your services. And it introduces your client servers and gives visitors a way to contact to them. It fulfills all of these functions via an attractive design that engages the visitor.

But that's not enough. Behind the scenes, you want your site to identify visitors, encourage their subscriptions to your content, and enhance their experience. A website that recognizes return visitors and welcomes them back or offers content similar to what they viewed the last time they visited is becoming more and more common. Soon it will be the norm.

Professional service firms can benefit from selecting a user-friendly website platform that does justice to the content that's produced. Written pieces, graphics, video, and podcasts are all elements in your publishing realm that can be used to present information to potential new subscribers. Having straightforward, easy-to-access, visually appealing content is key. Here are some questions to ask:

- When reading a piece of thought leadership, can a reader pause and resume later?

- Can a reader easily send to an article to a friend? (Do you get tracking?)

- How long did a reader stay on the page? (Was it long enough to complete the content?)

- Can all actions be recorded in your data ecosystem?

- Can you rank the published content for a period (week, months, year) based on popularity, open rate, or whether it was shared?

Content — the core tool that attracts attention to your firm

What attracts visitors to your site more than anything else? Content. Content may be in the form of written pieces, infographics, video, or podcasts. It's distributed via email, social media, and your website. (In the future, some firms will even launch web applications for their firm, similar to the news apps on your phone.)

Each of these considerations should be part of your content strategy:

- Packaging and search engine optimization (SEO). How do you organize and present your content so visitors and searchers can easily find and access it online?

- Tools to measure performance. How will you gauge success?
- A targeted distribution strategy based on your buyer persona and their preferred channels.
- Website tools that can allow gating content, collect visitors' email addresses, and recognize IP addresses of repeat visitors.

Subscription capabilities — tools and processes to organize and manage your subscribers

Subscriptions give more power to your thought leadership content by creating an annuity. Having a way to convert your one-time reader to a recurring reader depends on your subscription capabilities, and if the whole point behind thought leadership is to generate new business, this is an important capability. While it's conceivable that a reader may ask for a consultation after just one article, most will not. You need to nurture them until they recognize that you're uniquely qualified to help them. Getting your reader as a recurring subscriber will provide the ongoing opportunity to stay in front of your target audience.

Contact information — CRM and automation tools provide a 360-degree view of client/prospect interactions

A CRM (customer relationship management) system has many benefits for your firm, especially tracking contact with clients and prospects. When coupled with marketing automation software, CRM allows you to track information about your new subscribers, executed marketing and sales actions, results, subscriptions and more.

While many professional service firms have toyed with CRM, few would claim a strong ROI on their purchase. To get the full benefit, CRM should become the central intelligence system for your client contact information, firm connections, and subscription center. It should include practice development activities, pipeline, opportunities, records of staff activities for business forums, industry associations, volunteer opportunities and board seats. Otherwise, it's little more than a giant phone book.

Today, automation can take all of the mundane work out of keeping your CRM system up to date. In about 60 seconds a day, your client service team can update CRM from an email in their Outlook inbox using a system like Introhive. The technology will review calendars, phone records, and email, and ask staff to easily identify those which should be added to your CRM system. When a contact that's not in CRM is identified, a one-click option will create a new contact in CRM.

Lead generation and nurturing tools — the precursor to an appointment

Lead generation/nurturing tools involve marketing automation software guided by a combination of human and artificial intelligence to nurture prospects with thought leadership and get them ready for an appointment with a client server.

Human capital (Digital Scientist or Analyst) — making meaning out of data

This is someone whose sole job is to analyze your marketing data, look for potential clients, and create plans to improve engagement, nurture prospects, and move prospects through the early stages of the buying process. I'm calling this a scientist, because they're working with people's digital profiles.

Where there's data, there's complexity

When I was a kid, I remember watching a TV show called "Lost in Space," which was about a family who traveled through the galaxy trying to get back to Earth. I remember the captain sitting at his console as the ship would land or take off from different planets. He had control over the technology that allowed him to maneuver the ship at his fingertips.

Many professional service firms today are missing this person, the one whose sole job responsibility is to "manage the controls" and discover the secrets of their own digital marketing data. I call this role a data "digital scientist" or analyst. It's important that this is a stand-alone position because prospects slip through the cracks when we assign this task to everyone — but equip no one. (We've provided a generic job description in the appendix.)

I had a friend whose employer let all of their business developers go based on the premise that they'd use data to identify leads and rely on the client service team to follow up. While using data to identify leads is forward-thinking in one respect and a dedicated data scientist(s) can help drive more leads, eliminating the business development function may have been shortsighted. Seems they need to exist together.

The conventional thinking in many professional service organizations is that all administrative departments (non-client servers) are overhead, and these costs should be kept to a minimum to maximize partner profits. A selling feature for many of the digital tools is that they're a simple "bolt-on" to the tools already deployed, and no additional overhead is needed to take advantage of their new capabilities. You've heard the sales pitch before: great benefits and a low cost of operation. Some of you used this logic to build your digital toolset, but in my experience, the plan has backfired. Why? It's unrealistic to think we can delegate management of the complex data generated by these sophisticated tools to an existing position and expect it to get completed.

In addition to analyzing the volume of data that's generated, there's also the heavy weight of bad data. Data is a lot like freshly baked bread: if it's not stored properly, it can become stale very quickly. Data integrity, or lack thereof, also shows up when information is entered incorrectly, yielding typos, guesses about email formats, or data that changes after it was input. Both marketing teams and practice staff fall down on the job when it comes to correcting bad data. I've seen clients' names corrected multiple times on lists without anyone going into the source record to prevent it from happening again. Data cleansing, the term used to describe efforts to find and correct bad data, is a requirement that needs to be in your plans. Fortunately, there's automated software that can identify and suspend contact records with faulty elements; however, the most reliable method to fix the records lies with the client service team.

Another challenge that must be solved when using automated digital marketing tactics is gathering intelligence about the individuals attached to the IP addresses that hit your website. Usually, you're alerted when a single user from a company reads multiple articles. But what if multiple people from the same company each reads multiple articles? This may signal a more urgent prospect, especially as you delve into account-based marketing (tactics applied to multiple decision-makers in an organization instead of a single decision-maker). Most of the software on the market today can't identify the hidden patterns (and people) buried in IP addresses — but your data analyst can.

A related challenge is identifying and linking different IP addresses for the same user, a common situation that occurs when someone reads your content from both their work computer and their iPad. Who looks to see if they're the same person? Who combines the data and determines that both instances point to a higher level of interest than judged individually?

It's easy to ignore these challenges or address them on a catch-as-catch-can basis, but I'd argue that marketing teams should approach them proactively and holistically by incorporating a digital scientist as part of the digital marketing team. The digital scientist will live and breathe your organization's data, uncovering potential new clients along the way.

Introducing the digital data warehouse

For your digital scientist to be effective, they should have a proper "laboratory" or digital data warehouse specifically designed for marketing. The digital marketing warehouse, like other data warehouses, has data feeds from all of your tools and allows the data to be stored and manipulated to look for relationships that may not be readily apparent. Don't be put off for fear of a high price tag. Today, there are lower cost options that can give you an acceptable ROI. If you get 10 new clients instead of five, wouldn't it be worth it? As you build your digital ecosystem, this should be a tool you put in place toward beginning of your journey.

Your digital data warehouse gathers the universe of clients, prospective individuals and accounts, and referral sources that present your firm with opportunities to grow. The sooner you add a data warehouse and analyst capabilities, the sooner you'll get the full benefits of your own proprietary data — from your website and emails to webinar attendees and social media interactions.

Now, I wasn't an early believer in a data warehouse for marketing, but after trying to use our CRM system and various spreadsheets, I could never get all of the data feeds I needed from the data I already owned or have an adequate way to manipulate the data to uncover new prospects. The beauty of the warehouse is you get your data clean and in a rational configuration, but most importantly you get a platform that allows you to gain competitive advantage by unlocking relationships that your competitors missed — for instance, the ability to link two IP addresses to a single user.

To get the maximum value out of the data warehouse, you'll also need a digital scoring model, which is a point system that assigns values to your digital visitors based on the type of interaction, frequency, length of time, and even their propensity to share the content they read. A sophisticated system will accumulate a score at the account level, but less robust systems assign the score at the individual user level. You can design your system to alert the data scientist when certain scoring levels are reached. Reaching different scores can trigger specific actions, and hopefully, help you identify when it's best to introduce a human interaction. We found that when people reached our predefined score, we had a 25% chance that they'd accept a request for an appointment. A scoring model can help optimize your client servers' time by matching them with prospects at the most opportune time — not too early or too late. You can then avoid meetings that are pointless or premature.

Let's look at an example of a simple example of a "scoring model." Let's say Lisa found an article via a Google search that someone from your firm wrote. The article was gated, but the topic was especially important to her, so she gave us her email address and read the article. At the end of the article, she was offered a video on the topic that she also watched. Lastly, she went to your website and reviewed the bios of the two authors.

Using this scoring model, you'd award Lisa 25 points for reading the article and 35 points for viewing the video completely; you'd also award her 10 points each for the two bios she reviewed, bringing her total score to 80 points in a relatively short time. As a result of this score, it would make sense to call Lisa to see if she'd be interested in taking a telephone appointment with a representative of the firm.

Very often firm leaders may object to the cost of these "bells and whistles." I would offer that no professional services firm is setting the standard the way that companies such as Google, Amazon, and LinkedIn are. You need to get as close as possible or risk being dismissed as a lower-tier firm that's behind the times.

Closing thoughts about using digital marketing tools

We've talked about using the powerful ability of digital tools to attract and nurture a prospect along the buying path. The key is to create compelling content that's delivered in a variety of vehicles, including email, your website, and other sources like social media. By getting prospects to consume your content, you want to be able to:

- Offer them similar content, perhaps in a different format. For example, if a visitor reads an article on autonomous vehicles, they might like to sign up for a webinar on the topic.

- Offer visitors the ability to subscribe to the content they want.

- Create a scoring model that identifies when it's time for human interaction.

Digital tools in action

Through personal experience and discussions with my peers, I discovered that no matter how sophisticated any of the tools that we deployed were, their benefits would be limited if our marketing resources weren't trained and given the time to use all the features. Our strategy in selecting an email platform was to recognize that we would upgrade platforms as our team and needs got more sophisticated. Every two to three years, we reviewed our choices and upgraded to the next level. Our stairstep approach served us well, and the benefits were commensurate with what we paid.

That said, I did have colleagues who leap-frogged to the premium solution at the beginning of their journey and paid a premium price from the initial selection. However, when their team wasn't equipped to take advantage of all the advanced features, they paid for system capabilities that went unused. In the end, we both got to the same place, and there are lessons in both paths. The takeaway is to make sure you choose your path with your eyes wide open and create a digital roadmap that best allows you to fully take advantage of what you're paying for as soon as possible.

Finally, in today's world, you must be aware of cybersecurity tools and protocols that are designed to protect corporate environments. All your communications must be designed to maximize use in a cybersecurity-sensitive world. This adds new constraints. Ultimately, I think we'll end up with mobile apps for our clients and prospect's phones like the LinkedIn mobile app, but until that time we all need to keep this limitation front and center.

Summary

Your digital toolset should be designed with your firm's growth and success in mind. While many of the tools are sold for a single function, your marketing leader should be in a position to create an end-to-end system you can work toward to leverage all of data from disparate systems to your maximum benefit. Being able to use all of the data you collect should create a proprietary product that gives you an advantage.

Just like the saying that music happens between the notes, the best intelligence comes when you triangulate multiple sources. To take full advantage of your digital capabilities, dedicated resources and data warehouse functionality are mandatory. Working with a model that measures ROI as well as competitive positioning with your peers and chargeable hour increases will best position you for success.

GET OFF OF THAT DINOSAUR!

These questions will help you get out of The Stone Age and into The Digital Age. Ask yourself:

- Does your firm have a digital marketing strategy that can easily be explained to a recruit in one or two sentences?

- Does your marketing roadmap include technology due out in the next 12 months that isn't commercially available today?

- If you don't have the capability today to score prospects at the account level, do you have a clear path to get there?

- Does your marketing team have a performance metric focused on the number of leads generated by digital tools?

- Are your team members attending webinars and talking to vendors to stay on top of new technologies that may help you even more?

See Tool 5 for a sample marketing scientist job description.

"Thought Leadership Programs:" What Does That Even Mean?

Many professional service firms dedicate time and energy hunting for new clients that I refer to as "unicorns." Firms get their partners and staff whipped up to cold-call prospects in the hope of finding those mythical organizations that just happen to be looking for a service provider at the exact time the team is making their cold call. These "cold calling campaigns" may generate an appointment or two, but when the prospect doesn't buy on the spot, the opportunity is quickly written off as a failure. If the appointment hints at the opportunity for future work, only a few firms have the discipline to take full advantage of the situation and execute a vigorous follow-up plan. I wonder why firms replicate this process repeatedly, thinking that the next time will be different? Habit, I suppose, but today I want to talk about a better way.

If only...

If only you could gauge when a prospect is ready to pay for help from a firm like yours! If your prospects were like car buyers, you could link your outreach efforts to their three-year lease cycle.

Unfortunately, it's not that easy, but there's hope in the form of a thought leadership program.

Anyone who leases a car receives regular emails from their brand keeping them up to date about new features and new models. A thought leadership program does the same thing: it periodically presents the expertise of your partners and staff — in the form of written articles, podcasts, invitations to in-person events, round-tables, and webinars — to demonstrate your firm's capabilities and keeps you top of mind until they're ready to buy.

As an example, imagine a consulting firm whose expertise is internet security. The firm publishes a 10-question survey that helps the reader assess the various elements of their security infrastructure. That consulting firm is demonstrating their knowledge and commit-ment to help businesses fight cyberthreats — and that tool will likely elevate them in the eyes of their prospects.

This form of thought leadership accomplishes two things: (1) it helps prospects interpret their cyber risk, and (2) it gives them a preview of what it might be like to work with the cyber firm. Chances are that when the prospect is ready to address their cybersecurity issues, they'll solicit an RFP from the firm who prepared the survey.

Bottom line: Your "dream clients" want to work with thought leaders and will pay a premium to do so. If you can establish your firm this way in your prospects' eyes, you'll have an advantage when they get ready to make a purchase.

The beauty of thought leadership

The beauty of thought leadership is that it tracks alongside the buying habits of decision-makers who may become interested in your services. It keeps your firm top of mind without any of the annoying habits of a bad salesperson.

For example, most organizations create roadmaps for large expendi-tures in 12-month (or beyond) increments. Decision-makers at these organizations are constantly adjusting the roadmap for emergency projects that pop up (for example, a new patent issue, cybersecurity issues, or projects related to mergers and dispositions). They're also surveying their competitors to spot new technology that may improve efficiency, add new capabilities, improve communication, or make existing tools easier to use. They're constantly on the hunt for information that will keep their roadmap relevant and competitive.

A robust thought leadership program helps to inform the road-map by presenting emerging issues, new tools, and competitive strategies. Your thought leadership can position you as a strategic partner who may even deserve a premium price in the marketplace. So even if your service isn't required on the original roadmap, you may be able to heighten awareness and get the roadmap amended to include the capabilities you offer.

How does thought leadership create future buyers?

Thought leadership positions your firm as a subject matter expert that offers helpful advice. It should be easy to find and published on your website, in trade publications or association newsletters, and in paid LinkedIn posts — places your audience already visits.

Done right, it also had these benefits:

- Decision-makers will recognize you as a credible resource and keep you top of mind — for current and future buying decisions.

- It will create awareness and familiarize more potential clients with your expertise.

- It will entice organizations — those familiar with you and unfamiliar with you — to subscribe to your offerings, thereby adding to your proprietary database of prospects and clients.

- It opens the door for decision-makers to discover additional content that you offer: videos, print, podcasts, and more.

- It's a lead nurturing program for new and existing clients.

All it takes is one of the pieces in your program to attract a decision-maker's attention, and voila! You've started a digital relationship!

The ultimate goal is to create a lead nurturing program that generates a new client. Now, this may be a longer-term strategy than a cold-calling program, but it's probably 10x more effective. With the digital tools available, it's easier than ever and allows you to nurture your prospects without being pushy. When your marketing team comes to you with their plan, make sure a thought leadership program is among the considerations.

Not all thought leadership is good thought leadership

Your thought leadership program will only be successful if the content you're producing is interesting and professionally developed with a nod to the client's preferences. The content should be helpful to the audience. This is not the time to present puff pieces that brag about the firm.

To attract decision-makers, thought leadership should:

- Point to solutions that will improve their overall business results.

- Discuss future possibilities and how current decisions have interdependencies.

- Reflect an understanding of specific performance metrics that are pain points for their businesses.

- Improve their standing in their organization as a problem solver.

- Demonstrate that you "have their back."

In Chapter 2, we discussed developing the personas of an ideal client; a thought leadership program is a great way to make good use of that work. In both getting your articles published to a broader audience and attracting new audiences when publishing your own in-house proprietary publications, keeping the items your targets care about most front and center is critical to your long-term success. The more customized you are to your audience's interests, the better the articles will perform.

I often liken a successful thought leadership program to an experienced fly fisherman. (Disclaimer: I'm not a fly fisherman, but I had a boss who was, and I think it's a good analogy.) As I understand fly fishing, the key is to select a fly that's native to the geography on the day and time you're fishing. If you get this wrong, fish won't be drawn to your bait, and you won't be successful.

In a successful thought leadership program, you need to create content that's interesting and helpful to your specific audience. If you get that right, you'll be rewarded with a reader who subscribes to your newsletter and an elevated position in the eye of your clients. You'll get a higher level of attention and focus.

There should be a return for your investments

It took me a while before I realized that Plante Moran should have some return on all thought leadership we produced and that the bigger the investment to develop, the greater the expected return. I didn't want to use resources to create and publish content that we were giving away for free. I viewed our return in two ways. First, any request for new appointments and, second, new subscribers to any of our publications. I knew that our timing had to be impeccable to match the release of thought leadership with buyer decisions for that exact service; this probably wasn't realistic, but subscriptions kept our firm front and center until that timing aligned.

I remember the first time we established a lofty goal for a thought leadership campaign. We set a "ring the bell" goal of 400 new subscribers from a single campaign. I wasn't sure we'd make it, but by using many of the tools discussed in this section, we did. By my conservative estimate, the effort will eventually lead to more than $3,000,000 of new client revenue if only 5% of the new subscribers become clients.

It's okay to start small...and to curate content

A thought leadership program may begin with just one newsletter. That newsletter might serve you well for months, maybe even years. But as your subscriber base grows and becomes more diversified, you'll want to subdivide your subscribers into multiple publications of like-minded groups.

For instance, you could have one database of C-suite executives of automotive suppliers and another one of family office executives, offering custom content to each audience with information that's narrowly focused on the unique needs and interests of individuals with those common personas. I strongly advocate that your marketing team members and firm leaders work together to create as many channels (segmented instances of your proprietary contact information) that make sense for your readers and your business.

While most of the content will likely be developed by your firm or produced with a partner organization, some content may be purchased or what we call "curated" content. With curated content, you're offering content that may have been created by others but that you've approved or tailored for your audience. An example of curated content would be a tax update created by a content publishing firm that's offered along with a brief narrative that helps your audience interpret what they're about to read.

Don't forget about webinars and podcasts

Webinars and podcasts also qualify as thought leadership, so don't overlook them. They can effectively attract new audiences and demonstrate your firm's leadership and unique characteristics. Producing and publishing a podcast is a minimal-effort activity that just might be the bait you need to hook that big fish. If they like what you present and want to be among the first to hear about future podcasts, you scored a victory!

Webinars also give great flexibility. They can be video or audio-only and can be offered live or taped for on-demand airing. Webinars are nice for the people who considers themselves visual learners and get more out of a discussion than reading an article independently.

Driving performance and ROI of your thought leadership program

Today most firms deliver content to their subscribers via email, but soon it could be delivered to their phones through an application that operates like news outlets do today. No matter how it's delivered, there's a cost to create a new thought leadership program or deciding to customize content for a particular channel.

If you've determined there's a business case to justify a thought leadership program, there are at least five levers you can manipulate so your investment matches your expected return:

- Frequency of publishing
- Content type
- Number and length of articles
- The cost to recruit new subscribers
- Search engine optimization

In the end, you want to match your cost with the size of the potential.

Now, we're going to cover bullets 2, 3, and 4 in later chapters, but let's spend a few minutes on frequency and search engine optimization (SEO) now.

Frequency of publishing is a common way to adjust the cost of a thought leadership program. Readers will accept what you describe as your publishing schedule, but you need to stick to your stated cadence or risk losing interest. If your content is something that people really want, I would publish monthly or even more frequently.

You may want to use email open rates as a guide to how frequently you publish. In my experience, an open rate of 20% or less indicates the reader isn't very interested in the content. Open rates from 20–35% indicate that some readers are interested some of the time, and rates of 35–50% indicate the content is on target for and would justify at least monthly publication. If your open rates are over 50%, that means you're knocking it out of the park and should publish as often as you can because your audience is eagerly waiting for your next piece. (This may be a good indicator of a client wanting the service also.)

While your marketing team may cite national averages that say a 25% open rate is really good, I don't believe you should rely on these national averages as a guide. In the height of the COVID-19 pandemic when various government programs were being discussed, Plante Moran was seeing 55% open rates.

The same thought leadership that's published for subscribers will also do "double duty" as content for your website. Search engines will find it and bring in additional eyeballs, so you should make sure that the content is search engine-optimized. (Marketing professionals call this "SEO.") That way decision-makers (and their teams) will be offered your content during internet searches.

As we discussed earlier, your technology stack should include tools to track what people are reading and the frequency. It should help you evaluate the quality and popularity of what you publish so you can identify why certain pieces are popular and what's wrong with less popular content. It may not always be the content. It can be style, too. Look at articles that are published in your trade association newsletters or click on an ad in LinkedIn. Is the content formatted in a similar fashion to yours? If not, you may want to reevaluate.

Summary

Decision-makers are constantly rebalancing the future needs of their organizations. When done right, your thought leadership can influence those decisions while earning you respect as a subject matter expert.

As sellers, your challenge is to stay "top of mind" with decision-makers until they're ready for your services. A well-executed thought leadership program can do just that. It's a business version of the tortoise and hare scenario; the winner is the organization that finds a way to stay memorable and build their credibility until being hired.

A good, consistent thought leadership program will address the issues that are top of mind with your future clients: answers to business challenges, trends for the future, competitor updates, and issues that resonate with your prospects' buyers. It will help you raise awareness of your firm, increase your audience, and bring you opportunities that weren't available to you when your business development efforts could best be described as person-to-person combat.

GET OFF OF THAT DINOSAUR!

These tips will help you get out of The Stone Age and into The Digital Age:

Metrics you might review quarterly with your marketing lead include:

- Number of articles published in third-party venues.
- Number of website visitors from the published articles above
- Open rates for subscribers.
- Changes in each of these since the last review to surface both positive and negative trends.

See Tool 12 in the appendix for a sample checklist for content health.

Today's New Subscribers Might Be Tomorrow's New Clients.

In the last chapter, we talked about the benefits of a thought leadership strategy to attract new clients to your firm. With digital tools you can extend your publishing reach and get the content you produce in front of a larger and more targeted audience. You can show decision-makers that you understand their problems and nurture them until they're ready to make a buying decision.

A successful nurturing program relies on your ability to recruit new subscribers, those people who've told you that they like what you offer and want to receive more. Getting your content in front of an expanded list of decision-makers is crucial to successfully grow your subscriber list.

Only a small percentage of your readers will matriculate into new clients, so it's critical to build your list of subscribers. Let's assume a 5% annual conversion rate, meaning that 5% of your total subscribers will successfully move through the sales process and become a new client. This means you need 100 new subscribers each year to get five new clients. Most marketing teams will focus 90% of their energy on creating the thought leadership content and only 10% on planning to distribute it. But the distribution effort can be a bigger challenge than you think, so it's worth focusing at least 50% of your efforts on distribution — with the ultimate goal of expanding your subscriber base.

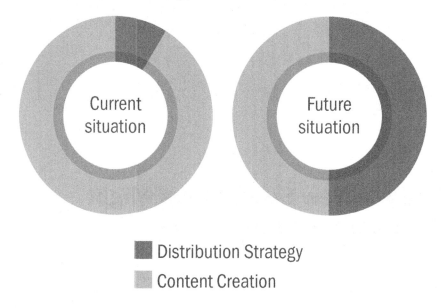

■ Distribution Strategy

■ Content Creation

To successfully create appealing content and distribute it to the most relevant audiences, you need two parallel projects. The first will be a deliberative approach to ensure that whatever you create resonates with the readers you're targeting and "breaks through" so that they want to read it. The second involves creating a robust distribution strategy focused on a clear definition of the groups of like personas that you've identified as your target audience(s); this includes the right publishing platforms, content distribution frequency, and budget considerations.

Creating thought leadership that attracts decision-makers

Creating a thought leadership plan that attracts new readers begins with choosing topics that are in demand. What are your clients' and prospects' biggest challenges? Are there opportunities they're missing out on? An internet search may help as well. You should also be able to count on your marketing lead to help vet potential topics to ensure your selections are compelling enough to attract a large readership.

Once you've settled on a strong topic, there are three goals to keep in mind:

- Attract the reader with your headline.
- Get the reader to read the entire piece.
- Entice the reader to subscribe to receive other pieces you publish.

In the next chapter, we'll dive deeper into how good content comes together, but let's cover a few basic steps to make sure you're off and running in the right direction.

Let's start with the title. Knowing how to title a piece is the subject of much debate in marketing circles, but the bottom line is this step deserves both attention and showmanship. Your title must attract the reader's attention, be compelling, and promise something new or undiscovered. If you think it sounds bland, the reader probably won't even notice it.

Think about it. We're bombarded with information all the time. Most of it is filtered out by our minds as "clutter" as a coping mechanism to deal with the overwhelming amount of information coming our way each day. Your clients and prospects are the same. If the title doesn't jump out, the piece will be relegated to the clutter file — never to be viewed again.

So how do you write a compelling title? By relating it to your readers' experiences. Something like, "Five overlooked tax tips that can reduce your tax bill," has an emotional benefit for the client. (Titles that include numbers tend to be particularly popular because the reader knows exactly what they're getting into.) Or "Mistakes most companies make when using social media," creates a natural curiosity around a nagging concern for many organizations. The point is the title must work hard to entice people to read the article. Often marketing teams will create a couple of titles, compare how they perform, and switch out to the best performing one. We call this "A/B testing."

This is an area where we can help each other. I know the importance of this subject, but my initial title for this book was still very bland. I originally had "A Marketing handbook for Nonmarketing Leaders." My intent was a no-nonsense title that promised the reader what I was delivering, but my team of draft reviewers torpedoed it immediately. I ultimately trusted my marketing colleagues who weren't as personally invested as I was to get more creative. Enter "Don't Ride a Dinosaur into Your Battle for New Clients and Other Lessons for Leaders Who Want to Grow their Business." It's a mouthful, but you can't deny that it got your attention!

Distribution strategies

To reach more readers who will find your content interesting enough to read and, ultimately, subscribe to, it's important to clearly define your target audience and document. This is often done via a creative brief that's drafted by marketing and agreed to by the authors of the individual pieces.

Then the team should brainstorm all the places where your targets might see and read the content. Marketing should lead an effort for the team to share their thoughts followed up by research into the digital and analog options for distribution, a plan, and budget.

I encourage you to dedicate at least 45–90 days to promote a piece of content. I've often heard pushback that this is too long, and the content will get stale. Unfortunately, while we might think a new piece will reach everyone in the intended audience immediately, it won't. It takes an extended period of exposure using multiple distribution tools for the maximum number of readers to be exposed to the piece. Don't make the mistake of changing pieces too frequently. (And if it starts to become outdated, update it. Updating existing content is a best practice anyway.)

When focusing on getting great content to as many new eyeballs as possible, there are many aspects to consider. The old-school method was to purchase email lists, send the content to the names on the list, and hope they opt in for more. Today's spam laws would strongly discourage us away from this path. The last thing you want is complaints against your firm and having your content flagged as "spam."

Instead, you want the security of knowing that subscribers have opted in to your emails. The following methods are acceptable ways to drive traffic to your thought leadership:

- Present it to existing clients. (They'll appreciate hearing your ideas, and it may result in new work. They may even send it to a friend.)
- Target executives in LinkedIn advertising.
- Offer it to visitors to your website.
- Get thought leadership published in national, association, and local business publications.
- Include a subscription offer in online or print ads that are produced.
- Ask staff to include a link to subscribe as part of their email signature.
- Offer it to people you meet while you're networking.
- Ask current subscribers to invite friends to subscribe.
- List "other pieces" the firm publishes in each publication. Perhaps under the banner, "You may also be interested in these other recent publications we shared."

We'll talk about LinkedIn in a later chapter, but publishing (sharing) the thought leadership produced should be a goal for everyone who works at your firm. Time and again, research has shown that people trust their friends more than the organizations they work for. Plus, the exposure is magnified. It's one thing if Plante Moran posts an article to its LinkedIn page — but it's significantly more powerful if the firm's 3,300 staff post it to theirs.

A few thoughts on digital advertising

Digital advertising should be a core element in your plan to attract new readers, but it can be tricky. Not only do you have to pick the optimal size and placement, but you need a standout call to action. Generally, the title of your thought leadership content is too long for digital ads, so you need a few, high-impact words to make a big impression. This is a skill in and of itself, and the sooner you acquire the skill on your team, the better.

The three most common options for digital advertising buys are based on:

- Impressions: This means that the digital ad is somewhere on a page that had a visitor; it doesn't mean anyone actually read the ad.

- Pay-per-click: This is a better indicator of the impact of the ad because visitors have to click on it to view it. I prefer the pay-per-click option, even though it's more expensive, because I can see how effective my ad was at catching people's attention.

- Retargeting: With retargeting programs, you're able to buy online ad space that will deliver a customized ad to people who have previously visited your website. For example, let's say a web visitor read the litigation section of your website. A retargeting program uses cookies to deliver ads about your firm once they've left your site. For example, if they visit CNN.com, they may see one of your ads. The ad is a reminder of your capabilities and hopefully it keeps you top of mind when they reach decision time.

Pay to play? Or not to pay to play?

As you delve into the thought leadership world, you may be tempted by the pay-to-play options that are out there. Pay-to-play generally means that you pay some dollar amount (usually big) to be a featured expert on a piece of content published by an established name. Usually, a business manager for some nationally recognized digital media reaches out on behalf of their named celebrity host.

The voicemail or email says you've been chosen based on your nationally recognized specialty in a certain area (exactly what a thought leader wants to hear). The caller makes it sound like a PR opportunity, and there's no mention about cost. When the call is returned, the seller lays out an expensive pay-to-play scenario. At Plante Moran, we never accepted these offers because it wasn't our model to pay for this type of media exposure. We also understood we weren't favored to come out the winner, and these offers were playing to our egos.

However, we did find a hybrid publishing opportunity that presented itself due to the changing field of journalism. With declining circulation and ad revenue, many publications have reduced their staff and are challenged to produce required content. We found a content creator who helped us develop "ready-to-publish" content that national publications would publish under contributor bylines that featured our experts. This created a win-win scenario for the publications and for our goal of extending the reach of our thought leadership. These national publications offered us an audience we couldn't have gotten ourselves.

One of the secrets about marketers is that we love to try new stuff! I'm more guilty than most. But jumping too quickly from one tactic to the next will be a diminishing return for any incremental efforts to add new subscribers to your thought leadership stream.

Summary

Getting a new reader is great accomplishment, but attracting a new subscriber is the ultimate goal. New subscribers can be very lucrative because you have a captive audience to show the benefit of your expertise and convert them into clients.

The value of this goal should be commensurate with the effort. This is an area that I think is perfect for continuous process improvement and experimentation. It isn't very expensive to either run side-by-side comparisons or to have sequential efforts. By trying different options to attract viewers — like tweaking the title, digital ad shape, or digital color — you may increase your readership significantly with little cost. As you experiment, you'll get better and better. If you get stumped, consider hiring an outside party for a single project to jumpstart your efforts with the goal of more subscribers. When you're successful, you can you emulate that success with your next effort.

GET OFF OF THAT DINOSAUR!

These questions will help you get out of The Stone Age and into The Digital Age. Ask yourself:

- If you had $10,000 more to recruit new subscribers, what would you try?

- What are five publication opportunities to get new subscribers that fit your ideal client that you don't use today?

- What three things can you do to make pay-per-click more effective for your organization?

- What are the common elements of titles that perform well for you?

- Where are your new subscribers coming from? How can you better leverage them?

10

Will My Mother Tell Me What I Really Need to Hear?

When marketers talk about digital campaigns, they like to say, "Content is king." That's true — as long as it's good content." But what is "good" content?

You and I could look at a piece of art and have a lively conversation about whether that artwork is "good "or not. Our opinions might be based on personal preference, the opinions of art experts, or whether we think the piece would look good in our living rooms. While there's room for personal taste when evaluating art, when it comes to evaluating the content that your organization produces, I urge you to expand your thinking a bit. Whether content is good or not depends on the intended audience — whether it captures their attention and causes then to view your firm as the preferred expert on the topic.

That's why I'm encouraging you, as firm leaders, to take the lead with your marketing teams and be deliberate and mindful about the subjects you address in your content. The danger is that, for most professional service providers, the content you're the most comfortable writing about isn't what's interesting to most readers. If you get the subject matter wrong, the content won't resonate with your audience, and the ROI will disappoint, despite your time and dollar investments.

Here are four things to keep top of mind:

- The subject matter must be important to your target audience.
- The content must be presented in a way that appeals to your audience.
- The subject must relate to a service your firm provides. (You're wasting money writing about something important to your client if your firm doesn't offer a service to address it.)
- Use your resources to produce pieces that are consistent with your firm's strategic direction. (Significant service lines get priority.)

Choosing the topic that resonates with your audience

When you start down the thought leadership path, you need to be involved in selecting the topic(s). I guarantee that even with a healthy review of the points above, the team's natural inclination will lead toward a "safe topic" — and good luck getting anyone to read it. Instead, you need to help guide the conversation and convey confidence in your team's ability to tackle more emerging topics.

Sounds great, right? But how can you educate yourself on potential topics? Start with simple Google searches like:

- Hot business topics
- Trending topics in … (insert your specialty)
- Top topics in industry publications (manufacturing, construction, healthcare, etc.)

You can also look at organizations in your field that have deep pockets to spend on research and production. Paying attention to recognized thought leaders like Fidelity, Salesforce, or Gartner is a good way to jumpstart your program and learn how they present their content in terms of:

- Topics
- Formats
- Length

At Plante Moran, we often formed editorial boards that were made up of partners and staff and a marketing team member who focused on a certain sector or service line to collectively choose topics for the thought leadership focus. I loved working with these teams to select and develop topics. I usually got a management team member to join the conversation, too, since they also saw the bigger picture. The more we did this, the easier it got for everyone as we developed a great sensitivity to what resonated with our audiences.

One great example occurred when data analytics was emerging as a field, and we had a breakthrough recognizing that these tools could provide pragmatic solutions to a wider variety of problems that our clients faced than we originally thought — from patient populations to inventory storage to store locations. That content attracted lots of readers and new subscribers.

Another tip: Think about how your specialty area affects your targets' personal lives. If your organization offers content applicable to both business leaders and individuals, mix it up and try offering content for the opposite audience.

For instance, the CIO is interested in the latest technology, but she may also be interested in something on estate planning. In another situation, donors might be interested in the exhibition schedule, but they may also be interested in content that was prepared for adults to share with their own children and grandchildren. Experiment and see if this cross-pollination can help and differentiate you from your competition.

One last thought that may give you an edge: I created a small group of outside advisors, which I'm guessing many of you also have at your disposal. I had a few personal friends in many of the demographics we were targeting; some were clients, and some were not, but I often used them as a stand-in for our real audience. A conversation over lunch, a quick phone call, or email easily put me in touch with their thinking. When you bring input vetted by potential audience members, your thoughts as marketers will carry a lot more weight in the conversation.

Tips to make your content stand out and hold attention

With so much other content competing for your readers' time and attention, you want your content to stand out. We've talked about how important the title is to get the reader to open the article, so now let's move on to format.

The rules we learned about story composition in our sixth grade English class are out the window now. Today, we need to move the conclusion that was revealed in the last sentence of the last paragraph all the way up to the front. This is the "inverted pyramid" style of writing favored by writers, journalists, and content creators that begins with the most important elements of the story to draw in readers — and then keep their attention. You can easily lose your reader one sentence into the piece if it doesn't seem like it will be worth their time.

Inverted pyramid style of writing

Most important information
Conclusion:
Crucial information the reader should know

Additional information
Supporting detail to help the reader understand the main idea

Nice to know
Additional background info

In the remainder of the article, you can then describe problems that will result when the stated conclusion isn't properly addressed, how those problems can be identified, and a peek at the path to improvement. (This is crucial. You don't want to offer a step-by-step plan; you want prospects to hire you, not do it themselves.)

We've found that, today, content that takes more than 3–5 minutes to read is often abandoned, meaning the reader stops reading before the end. The one exception to this rule may be your technical buyer, who loves the details, so you may want to offer an extended version with more details for this reader. However, for most decision-makers, the traditional "white paper" is the kiss of death.

This is an area where old habits die hard — for years, "white papers" were a sign of high-quality and in-depth investments by firms. But despite the fact that none of us read them anymore, we still have partners whose go-to answer is, "We need a white paper." This preference has changed and should be reflected in the updated personality profile of your target personas. I'd go so far as to say that when I'm reading an interesting piece of content, if it isn't wrapped up in the fifth paragraph, I'm negotiating with myself about the benefit of continuing or abandoning it under the false pretense of coming back at a later time. I'll bet you're similar.

By presenting content that's hyper-tailored to your audience and sensitive to the demands on their time, you'll earn their trust, attention, and loyalty.

There are lots of formats out there, use them correctly

This same advice applies to thought leadership that's produced in formats besides print. If it's video, a well-thought-out, two-to-three-minute video is best. After three minutes, attentions start to wane, distraction sets in, or other communications begin to compete for the viewer's time. It would be a shame to have a prospect's attention for three minutes but lose it at minute four just when key points are being made.

But what if you have content that's longer than three minutes? Break it into segments. This allows you to tell the full story, but in manageable bites.

With webinars, audiences have been trained to expect longer content, so you have some flexibility, though webinars for C-suite executives should stay within the 30-minute range. Even so, you never want one talking head for an entire 30 minutes. There are numerous visual techniques to break up a talking head during a video, including graphics, PowerPoint slides, additional speakers, and audience Q&A.

I realize that some professional service firms offer 50-minute webinars that are eligible for continuing professional education. The longer format may be great for referral sources and people who may be supporting the decisions to hire professionals and are maintaining some type of certification, but I still wouldn't recommend the longer length for C-suite executives though.

You also want to make sure that all of your thought leadership is easy to share. If the audience can't share with colleagues, friends, and family, you aren't getting the full return on your investment. When you understand that most corporate decisions are made by five or more people, the ability to share content is a great advantage. Making sure you have this capability can help you convert more decision-makers to clients.

We've said that getting a reader to subscribe is one of the top prizes in a thought leadership program, only to be topped by a request for an appointment! So have you made it easy to subscribe? Have you given your audience multiple opportunities to subscribe or request an appointment? Instead of placing these offers only at the end of the piece, how about also including them early on, just in case prospects are enjoying the content but don't read until the end.

Summary

As a leader, your job is to make sure your teams are stretching and producing content that your audience will consider relevant. Don't let partners' egos or comfort zones color what your audience wants to read.

Update content formats to capture the audience's attention. You're not trying to get a good grade from your sixth grade English teacher; you want more business.

Finally, use resources wisely. Creating good thought leadership takes time. Make sure your strategic growth areas get resources before they're disbursed to less important areas. Sometimes the smallest practices will be the first to ask for resources, and it's usually difficult for a marketing team member in a professional services firm to tell a partner "no."

GET OFF OF THAT DINOSAUR!

These tips will help you get out of The Stone Age and into The Digital Age:

- Track the top open rate of thought leadership pieces.

- Track abandonment rates. What pieces have readers leaving after 10 seconds?

- Track the percentage of viewers who shared content with others.

See Tool 12 in the appendix for a sample checklist for content health.

11

The Golden Gate Bridge is Popular. Gating Content...Not So Much.

Ever had to fill out a form on a website to access a piece of content? Then you've experienced "gated content."

"Gating" is the marketing practice that requires people to provide their personal information — typically name, organization, and email address before they get carte blanche access to your thought leadership. It's the cyber equivalent of a privacy fence.

Most website software records the IP addresses of visitors to a website. When the IP address is from a corporate environment, you can tell that someone from ABC company has visited, but you won't know who specifically. And if they enter from their home computer, you'll only know that someone from a massive web provider like Comcast has visited.

The gating process links actual people to website visitors, and because website software stores browsing history from an IP address, you can also begin to build a profile about their interests. (Ideally, today's technology would enable you to link that same person and their website patterns across all their devices and then combine them as one in your data warehouse. This is still a new frontier in most professional service firms' digital ecosystems, but it's solvable with the right resources.)

What to do about buyers who don't want to surrender their contact information? One technique that's often used is to offer a "teaser" before any contact information is required. This is where that "strong opening statement" that we described in the last chapter comes into play. By offering the reader the opening paragraph as "ungated" material, it works as a loss leader for the rest of the content. If the opening is strong enough, the reader will provide contact information in order to see the rest.

The relationship is transactional

When a visitor gives you their email address, they're aware that they're giving you something of value. So when you decide to gate your content, the onus is on you to prove that you're offering them something of equal value and to deliver on the promise. This is where the value the reader places on our content has a heightened importance. Are you writing about something that's new or fresh? Does your title quickly and capably accentuate the benefits hidden behind the gate? Gating is where the rubber hits the road when it comes to offering content that will drive success in your digital marketing programs.

In the spirit of continual process improvement, track the number of visitors who abandon your site when they discover that some type of contact information is required. By tracking and trying to refine the elements, you can fine-tune your approach and become more effective in how your present your content in front of the gate.

To gate or not to gate?

Philosophies about gated content have evolved as web visitors have evolved. There are a lot of marketing gurus out there who say that gating is a thing of the past and that today's internet engines demand equal access for all, but the same firms who advocate these positions often gate their content for new clients.

In my opinion, in today's world, having all ungated content is like throwing $100 bills out of a car window. If you create interesting content and title it effectively, you'll attract interested buyers.

And it doesn't have to be an all-or-nothing proposition. You can gate the premium content you publish and not gate more generic webpages that describe your services or other information you may publish like a payroll tax schedule.

Some firm leaders think that gating makes them look like small potatoes. Wouldn't any big firm have a lot of material to give away for free as an investment? I think this is a remarkably interesting conversation filled with contradictions. Our goal is to attract a lot of high-quality potential buyers. It will take experimentation to see what's right for each firm.

Open the gate for known visitors

A very important "note to self" when adopting a gating strategy is to make sure your current clients and good referral sources have easy access to your content. Either put them on an exception list that continues to grant access or enact a one-time registration process. Both can work, but a good communication plan is key so everyone knows what to expect. And as your website technology evolves and starts to recognize known visitors, access to the gated content will be seamless because the system will recognize them.

Final thoughts

For me, leading our team through the conversation to gate was a long one with many twists and turns. Many of our marketing team members didn't want to gate any content; some were willing to gate some content, and others wanted to gate everything. With lots of conversations and some persuasion, we got everyone to abide by similar guidelines.

When you have multiple decision-makers owning different parts of your site, you need to negotiate an acceptable solution for all so that visitors have a similar experience, regardless of what pages they visit. When you begin this journey, plan on a bit of dialogue, and come prepared with what industry leaders and competitors are doing. Give people permission to try something new, and acknowledge that, with any well-thought-out idea, there's still some risk of failure — but the reward outweighs the risk.

Summary

You wouldn't routinely give away free advice when others are paying for similar advice, right?

Gating content is the exchange of your valuable intellectual property with a prospect's even more valuable — information. Many sophisticated people today expect to give contact information if they're getting something of value. By not asking for information, you may be telegraphing that you're not offering anything substantial. But if you're going to gate, make sure your content is worthy of the information you're requesting. Experimenting with the format and approach will help you get the best results.

GET OFF OF THAT DINOSAUR!

These tips will help you get out of The Stone Age and into The Digital Age:

- Talk with marketing to see what process they're following to match commercial email services to personal email addresses.

- For gated content, track the abandonment rate by article. What best practices that will lower the abandonment rate?

- Make partners who advocate for not gating content justify their reasons before agreeing.

- Track the unsubscribe rate. If poor content is the cause, that may have unintended consequences that should be addressed.

- A good transition plan for clients and referral sources when adopting a gating strategy is crucial.

12

You Won't Know Who's Winning Without a Scorecard.

Have you ever visited a website and, while you were looking around, your phone rang — and it was a salesperson from the company whose site you were on? Or, have you ever downloaded a white paper and received a sales call soon after?

Tactics like these may seem creepy and a bit desperate, but the marketing automation technology behind them can be a powerful tool in your digital arsenal. These technologies give you insights into the activities of people who are visiting your website and consuming your thought leadership. At some point in a prospect's journey, their actions may signal a readiness to buy that you don't want to miss. It's up to you to decide when and how to interact with your digital visitors and, just as importantly, how to avoid coming across as a digital stalker.

A developed scoring model will help you balance visitors' buying signals and overzealous sellers' missteps. Lead scoring allows you to assign point values for various visitor interactions with your online content. Through your scoring model, you track the activities of people who've identified themselves to you and then trigger a personalized touchpoint when they reach a defined score. As a reminder, these are people who have identified themselves by subscribing to your content, attending a webinar, providing an email to read gated content, or even responding to an advertising offer for a white paper download. In other words, they've shown interest in your organization.

As an example of how this works, we used our marketing automation software and created a scoring model that alerted us when prospects reached 100 points in a six-month period. At 100, the prospect would receive a call from our telemarketing firm asking for a meeting with members of our practice staff. The recipient could never track the call to any specific action on their part, but their interactions demonstrated they had a high interest in us.

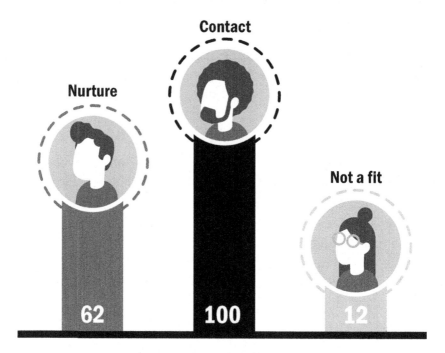

You can use scoring for more than deciding when it's time to reach out for a meeting with a prospect. You can use the scoring model and marketing automation technology to nurture prospects along the decision process, too. For instance, if a prospect reaches a score of 25, how can you get them to 50 points more quickly than they went from zero to 25? By finding their trigger points, you may be able to shorten the sales cycle and better position your firm.

It's also important to remember that the scoring model is two-dimensional. In addition to the points assigned for different activities, there's a time factor. If someone reaches 100 points in three years, they're probably not as strong a buyer as someone who reached the same point in four months. Your model needs to take both factors into account.

But how do you know which of the people who are interacting with your thought leadership are valid buyers? After all, the content you offer could attract attention from any number of people: prospects, clients, employees, potential employees, competitors, referral sources, job seekers, students doing research, or other random people.

It may take a little research, but you should be able to assign these groups to the appropriate buckets. For competitors and nonqualified buyers, I suggest you assign them a score of negative 250 to get them out of your consideration set. You can send job seekers to your HR team, and current clients can be sent to the engagement team.

Example of a lead scoring path

A qualified buyer — let's call her Mindy — gets her first introduction to your firm and attends a webinar. The next week you offer her an article on the same topic. After she's read a few articles, you offer a complimentary 30-minute conversation with the author. All the while Mindy continues to accumulate points as she consumes more and more content — and your data scientist is monitoring her, every step of the way.

As she works her way through the process to hit the predefined score in your model, your data scientist can do one of three things:

- Have a telemarketing firm call and try and set up an appointment (possibly a Zoom call to make an introduction and understand Mindy's needs). When they get an appointment, the business developer steps in and creates a small group to meet with her.

- Notify a business developer, who'll try and set up a meeting.

- Notify a partner or practice staff to set up an appointment.

My preferred method is option one. It's more efficient to use the telemarketing function to arrange the call because it may take several attempts, and the person who's deep into your thought leadership may not be the person to authorize the meeting. An appointment setter is best suited to manage this step.

Cohorts can be helpful

Before sending a lead to telemarketing, our practice was to place companies that scored high and passed through all the approvals into two different cohorts:

- Not a client but someone in the firm knew them or knew someone at their company. When there was a valid connection in CRM, we gave the lead to the person at the firm who had the connection. In my view, this was a "payback" for putting contacts into the system. The person had 10 days to contact the lead and document it. If there was no entry in CRM, we sent the lead to our telemarketing firm to try and get an appointment. If we were successful, we'd loop the firm connection back in at that time.

- Not a client and no reference point exists for them in CRM. If a lead wasn't a client and didn't have any connection in CRM, we'd send them to the telemarketing organization to try and set up an appointment. We had an extremely high conversion rate with these contacts.

I'd recommend following suit. We always created a team where a business developer and one or more practice staff collaborated

124

to convert the lead. This way, a business developer could carry the effort when the practice staff were serving other clients and the prospect wasn't yet at their decision point. By involving the business developer and the practice staff, the prospect got the attention they deserved and the technical advice they needed, when they needed it. To ensure full cooperation, we gave full credit to both the business developer and the team to ensure there were no territorial issues. Any additional commission was more than offset by the higher growth rate of new clients.

Remember to account for multiple visitors from one organization

When you build your lead scoring model, you must also make sure that it aggregates multiple visitors from the same company. When multiple people from one company, read your content, and attend your webinars, I take this as a particularly good sign about how that company views your firm. Your software should be able to account for a situation where there are multiple visitors from an organization, even if no one person triggered a lead score. It may be a good bet that your firm is being talked about, and you should make your way to the inside.

Beware of false positives

False positives are a real thing. If you ever took a statistics class, you learned about beta error. Because false positives can scramble your buying signal, I recommend that you run the model for at least 4–6 months to calibrate it before placing any great reliance on the data. If you find that none of the prospects who triggered your scoring model wants an appointment when you reach out, obviously calibration is necessary. Or if, after meeting with the prospect, you find they weren't good candidates, make modifications.

Whatever method you choose, it's important to eliminate as many of the non-buyers as possible. Can you imagine the fatigue and distrust you'd cause if someone in your firm reaches out, only to find most of the leads are either current clients or unqualified buyers? I often see this with webinars when partners want all the attendees called. I urge you to be cautious and review attendees before you involve anyone in follow-up calls. It's much easier to just offer seminar/webinar attendees the opportunity to raise their hand for a free, follow-up consultation.

Keep an eye out for duplicate data

Using a customized scoring model can be a great help; it can also identify past sins.

I'd never been someone who invested much of my limited budget in cleaning up duplicate organizations in CRM. Many staff who wanted to enter data into CRM would set up the organization to record their activity and would generally ignore the system warning that that organization already existed there. At one point, we were creating 90 duplicates a week.

The scoring model cured me of my tendency to ignore this problem because, if you have two organizations that may be getting activity points instead of one, you can easily mask the real client engagement because it's split between two entities. It's very embarrassing to call and ask a client for an "introductory appointment" (OUCH, right?!). Once we implemented lead scoring, we took a daily approach to eliminating duplicates and the problem went away.

Perfecting the lead scoring model

When it comes to your scoring model, you can't just set it and forget it. It's important to periodically reevaluate your model to make sure it's working for you.

When I started this journey, there weren't many models to follow, and I made more than my share of mistakes. I started with thousands of lines downloaded from our CRM system; for two weeks, I worked with an assistant to just try and make sense of what we had and how to organize it. By digging into the details, I identified the first round of challenges and understood some of the issues with our data.

For instance, when we first started, I discarded all of the non-corporate email addresses because I rationalized that they were either job seekers or not serious buyers. However, as our research went on, we found that our decision-makers were often visiting our site from multiple devices and that the discards could be engaged buyers. We then revised our policy and worked to establish them as prospects or link them to other business accounts that we'd already established.

Lastly, you may want to have a sales funnel specifically for the leads that come from the scoring model to track as a group. You can look at various methods to try and close new business, like free consultations, special access to firm experts, or a small event with some firm clients. You're looking for levers to use for this highly engaged group that might be different than other prospects due to their involvement with your firm.

Summary

By creating a scoring model, you can easily segment the engagement of your prospects and create a workstream to tailor the best path to convert them to clients. In some cases, your workstreams will work to pull the leads through your sales pipeline. The scoring model can also help you avoid wasted efforts for nonqualified parties and more precisely determine when human interaction is appropriate. You can further define the type of human interaction among your telemarketing service, business developer, and practice staff to get the best result and avoid unnecessary distractions for your client service providers.

GET OFF OF THAT DINOSAUR!

These tips will help you get out of The Stone Age and into The Digital Age:

Possible metrics to measure success:

- Number of leads sent for appointment setting
- Number of appointments
- Tailored scorecard to determine what score is most associated with a prospect who's agreeable to a higher level of engagement and what score is appropriate for the greatest chance of a prospect accepting an appointment.

13

World Wide Web, Faster
Than a Speeding Train.

Never has your organization been more connected to the global community. By and large, that's a good thing. But just as the web makes it easy to find you, it also makes it easy to leave you.

Websites are often referred to as the "digital face" of a company. So — what does yours look like when prospects come calling? Is it put together? Or does it look like it just crawled out of bed?

A website has multiple purposes. Its most basic role is to let visitors know what your firm does and the type of clients you serve. It likely starts with a "homepage" that's designed to give an overall view of your firm, and it may include a statement about the impact you want to have for your clients. Visitors navigating through the site will find pages on the various industries you serve and the types of services you offer as well as information about your locations, qualifications of and contact information for your partners, and current job openings. It may even discuss your inclusion & diversity or community service initiatives. The larger the firm, the more complex your website will be.

If you've surmised anything from reading this book so far, it's that your website is also the digital doorway that leads to business development opportunities. Your thought leadership will attract visitors, and your site gives visitors a chance to get to know your firm better and obtain more of your thought leadership through your subscription services. Organizing this information in a rational way takes skills that can't be easily overlooked.

However, most people working in professional services don't understand the path these website visitors follow. When you enter a house, you enter from one of the doors, but imagine a world where you could land in a kitchen without ever coming through an outside door! Your website visitors do this all the time. Sure, they can enter from your homepage, but probably 80–90% of your visitors start on an interior page. Why? Because they come in via a search engine like Google.

Search is the helicopter that drops website visitors exactly at the destination they've chosen. If you need proof, investigate your website data. It can easily tell you where visitors arrive, and you'll gain a new appreciation for their digital path.

But that doesn't mean your partners will — at least not initially. I frequently heard my internal clients say that it took too many clicks to get to the page that described what they did at the firm. They understood that the complexity of the firm required a complex navigation structure, but they wanted to be an exception to the rule so their visitors could find them easier than others' services. They believed that if it took more than 3–4 clicks to get to their page, their business development efforts would be impaired.

The counter argument, however, is that where pages are in the hierarchy had little bearing on their visitors because SEO (search engine optimization) typically delivered visitors in one click. Our research showed that even when people knew our web address, they used their search engine 95% of the time. This may defy logic to the T-rexes and stegosauruses among us, and it may even be contrary to how the people complaining find information on the web, but it's the truth. Don't waste time and money trying to solve a problem that only exists in eyes internal to your firm. It may be easy to blame web hierarchy for lack of business, but a better version of the truth is the lack of thought leadership (or quality thought leadership) that the target audience wants to read.

In our current world of SEO, most prospects will find their way to your website because you've published some type of thought leadership that they want to explore. I was always surprised at how many of our website visitors came to our site through a Google search — at times it was over 80%. The search engine robots constantly crawl the internet and index your content. Chances are each page on your website is indexed, so even if you don't have thought leadership, the pages describing your services and people still reside in the search results. Once your pages are included, how high you rank is based on a constantly changing set of criteria that your marketing team will have to become proficient at executing. Or you can easily hire experts.

Search practices of web visitors

I like to categorize website visitors into five main buckets based on their web usage patterns:

- Prospects
- Clients
- Competitors

- Future employees
- Companies looking to qualify your company for RFP submission

Prospects usually come in through a website search for a specific service or problem topic. Generally, when they click the Google link, it will take them directly to the content they want to review, regardless of how many clicks it is from the homepage. Therefore, **the number of clicks doesn't matter for prospects; what's important is helpful thought leadership and compelling content.**

Once you've invested in thought leadership, it's just as important to understand SEO compliance, which is an ever-changing discipline. Google, the "big dog" of search, continually changes its search algorithms so people can't manipulate the system or prevent their search engines from displaying valuable results. SEO takes expertise, so if your firm doesn't have it, hire it.

Competitors and future employees are two groups who have an abundance of time. They typically start on your homepage and leisurely work their way through the site. They're interested in the end state and what they learn along the way. The competitor is working to create a dossier on your firm. Future employees are looking for context for upcoming interviews.

People who are trying to qualify your firm to submit an RFP may also start at the homepage. Generally, the decision maker has delegated this task to a staff they've asked to qualify potential service providers. If they find the service offerings they're looking for, you'll get an RFP.

In other cases, someone in their company may have raised your name as an option, and the company needs to follow good purchasing protocols, which require multiple bids. When you receive an RFP and don't know the company, they may just need a quote from you to meet purchasing requirements so they can hire the party they wanted to hire anyway. (By the way, it's a good idea to create criteria to evaluate when you reply to RFPs.)

All that said, you want to make submitting an RFP invitation as easy as possible. I suggest a big "submit RFP" button on each page. I will add a caveat that will be discussed in greater detail in the chapter on proposals: In today's digital age, you need to take extra steps to identify people you don't know in person but who are reading your thought leadership. You may not recognize the company name that's submitting the RFP, but if you look at webinar attendees, subscribers, and people who have downloaded content, you may have a match, which may indicate a greater chance of winning the work than you originally suspected when you didn't recognize their name.

Websites require a substantial annual investment, and spending wisely is important. Understanding who your visitors are and how they use your site can help you make investment decisions. Armed with this information, I once deferred redoing the homepage and invested instead on improving the functionality of the page that housed our thought leadership. If few people start at the homepage, did I really care if our competitors saw the same page a few years in a row? I weighted prospects over competitors, which is extremely easy when you're making fact-based ROI investments.

Amplify your online presence

There are numerous other opportunities to extend your digital presence, especially in search engines. For example, don't overlook your digital address. As you know from your own search habits, the top couple of offerings when the search results are returned are paid spots. This means that your competitor can (and many do!) buy advertising rights to your organization's name, and when someone googles the name, their name may show up in the first position. As a defensive move, many companies are buying ads for their own names in search engines to guarantee they show up at the top of the page.

Another digital opportunity for your website visitors is called retargeting, which we mentioned in Chapter 9. This allows you to place digital ads on other sites to remind your visitors about your firm.

Suppose someone comes to your website to read a piece of thought leadership but doesn't subscribe to your newsletter. Even after they leave, you have an opportunity to recruit them to subscribe or deliver other messages. This is accomplished with a simple piece of code and is relatively inexpensive. I suggest that you discuss this option with your marketing team.

Summary

As a firm leader, you may ask staff, "What do you think of our website?" To answer you, most people will go to the homepage and search around the site. This is an artificial tour that's not indicative of how your prospects interact with your site.

You have the opportunity to work with your marketing team and use credible data to show how your visitors are getting to your site and how they're navigating while there. This is powerful information and should drive your website investments. Realizing that your website experience starts in the search engine and extends beyond the signoff to retargeting ads throughout the internet will position you for greatest success.

 GET OFF OF THAT DINOSAUR!

These tips will help you get out of The Stone Age and into The Digital Age:

- Create a metric that tracks how many of your services appear in the top 10 spots for non-paid searches.

- Track who's buying your name for paid search advertising.

- Rely on the data your website produces to benchmark your own progress.

14

Just Google Me!

In early 2017, I was on a plane leaving New York City and headed to Fort Lauderdale, Florida. Shortly before takeoff, a tussle ensued in first class, and I heard one of the passengers say to the other, "Let's google each other and see who's more important."

That was the first time I'd heard anyone use that phrase to settle a disagreement about who had the upper hand, and fortunately it was the last. But it does indicate the growing influence of our digital personalities — especially on social media.

If you're one of those people who thinks social media is a waste of time, please keep reading. Beyond industry conferences, networking breakfasts, and Zoom meetings, in today's business world, social media sites are quietly revolutionizing how and where we're able to network. These platforms, especially LinkedIn, are providing a competitive advantage to professionals who've figured out how to use them for network building and business development.

Let's discuss the benefits of social media tools for practice partners and staff, the marketing function, recruiting, and other administrative areas. If this is new to your firm, heads up because I'll encourage you to lead by example!

The fact is, many of your targets use Facebook, Instagram, Twitter, and LinkedIn. Here are some stats about these platforms from Sprout Social:

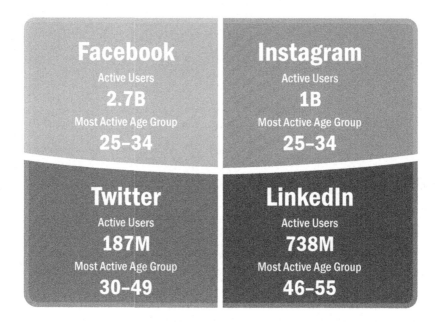

Facebook	Instagram
Active Users	Active Users
2.7B	**1B**
Most Active Age Group	Most Active Age Group
25–34	**25–34**
Twitter	**LinkedIn**
Active Users	Active Users
187M	**738M**
Most Active Age Group	Most Active Age Group
30–49	**46–55**

Facebook is generally for personal use and is best used as a platform for talking about firm culture and to show job openings. It isn't a tool in the B2B world. The only exception would be services your firm offers for individuals and their households, like wealth management, tax planning, and home cybersecurity. In those instances, Facebook may have benefit for you.

Instagram, like Facebook, is mostly aligned with personal use and is great to showcase firm culture and job openings, especially for campus recruits. Similar to Facebook, its demographic is younger, but these folks are your prospects' future leaders, so it's wise to connect with them early.

At Plante Moran, we used Twitter more to connect with media, but it's also a good platform to feature your firm's thought leadership.

And then there's LinkedIn, the primary social media tool for white-collar business professionals in a B2B capacity, and the topic of the rest of this chapter.

Making the most of LinkedIn

As the primary social media tool for business, LinkedIn is used to:

- Establish your personal identity in the business community.
- Publish thought leadership to decision-makers in your network.
- Research how to bridge your connections to businesses you want to meet where you don't have a direct contact.
- Highlight previously unidentified connection points that could lead to potential new clients.
- Research potential business targets.
- Advertise to micro-targeted geographies and job titles.

Establish and maintain connections with your network

The central function of LinkedIn is to create a network. At a minimum, everyone in your firm should be connected. You should also consider sending LinkedIn invitations to your Outlook contacts, including clients and prospects. After each meeting with a new contact, as you add their name in CRM and Outlook, send them a LinkedIn invitation.

You might ask, why put them in CRM and Outlook and still send a LinkedIn invitation? Remember how difficult it is to keep contact information current? In LinkedIn, it's the responsibility of the LinkedIn participant to update their information. LinkedIn will help when your data becomes stale due to job moves and mergers.

I started my relationship with LinkedIn a few years before joining Plante Moran in 2007. At first, there was some reluctance to use it — a popular social media platform, Next Life, had recently folded, and partners were afraid LinkedIn would follow a similar path. I was candid with them. I told them that yes, it very well may get eclipsed, but that didn't make their adoption any less urgent because LinkedIn had become a competitive advantage.

In a little bit of tongue-in-cheek advice, I offered that any partner retiring in the next five years could ignore the tool if they chose, but people who had a longer horizon should adopt it or risk their own obsolescence. The future was certainly not as dire as I predicted, but I have heard prospects say that, in their search for new professionals, as part of the decision process they looked up everyone from every firm they were considering on LinkedIn, and the results made an impression and informed a decision.

Publish thought leadership and demonstrate your expertise

We're all bombarded with content, from the media and emails, to professional and business journals. Some of it's good content, some is not so good and, today, some may even be fake. That's why content from trusted sources is more valuable than ever.

Study after study shows that people trust content from those that they know, so imagine the reach of your firm if every team member were to publish firm content — linked from your website — to their personal LinkedIn network. Thousands of decision-makers would be interacting with your content and trusting it in a way that just wouldn't happen if it were from your firm alone. This can result in tons of new website visitors and content subscribers. Again, the end goal is to get new work, which usually takes multiple impressions. LinkedIn can help.

Identify and validate prospects

LinkedIn can also help you identify potential prospects where you have multiple contacts, both directly and indirectly. Since LinkedIn gives you access to your network's contacts, you can easily identify people who may be able to introduce you to prospects where your only path had been cold calling. Even if the link isn't to the decision-maker at a target company, the warm entry might be enough to get a positive start to your pursuit. With LinkedIn, you may be able to identify good prospects that are right under your nose.

Early in this chapter I suggested that social media is a tool for everyone at your firm. I can't emphasize this enough. We all have networks. It may be a pipeline of new employees, referral sources, or prospects. The more connections your partners have, the closer you are to new business.

LinkedIn can also be a powerful educational tool. It gives every-one — clients, prospects, and staff — an opportunity to see what thought leadership your firm is publishing and educate them about your services. It's also a great opportunity for your internal teams to share current topics in their practice, whether it's IT, marketing, HR, or internal accounting. This kind of exposure can increase the general business knowledge of your team and elevate them in the eyes of their clients.

YOUR LINKEDIN CHECKLIST

I know what you're thinking: "Jeff's absolutely right. I need to do more on LinkedIn. But where should I start?" Here are some recommendations.

1. **Create a unique public profile that showcases your personality and tells people what you do.** Be sure to include a professional photo. That profile will generally rank at the top of internet searches because LinkedIn is so well-scored by search engines.

2. **Be sure to include all of your titles.** If you're in a multi-office firm and you lead a sector for your office, be sure to include it, don't be shy. Office-level titles sound just as impressive to the outside world and will elevate you against competitors who don't have a similar title.

3. **Tell stories about your successes.** You can use long-form posts for this purpose. This will establish credibility and trust as well as educate your network about firm services.

4. **Post your firm's thought leadership.** I would recommend posting 2–3 times per week.

5. **Share additional thought leadership that pertains to your practice.** As long as it's not coming from a competitor, sharing third-party content is perfectly acceptable — welcome, even. (It shows that not everything is "about you.")

6. **Be social.** Like and comment on your colleague's posts. If you download LinkedIn to your phone, you can do some of these activities at the kids' soccer practice or the doctor's office waiting room.

7. **Identify targets.** Look at your network and identify the people you think could best benefit from your services — and then engage them.

8. **Ask for recommendations.** LinkedIn allows others to endorse skills, so don't be shy about asking close colleagues to put in a good word for you. The more specific, the better.

Summary

Social media can be your firm's new secret weapon, but only when it's embraced by all. As a leader, set an example by connecting to others, posting articles, and acknowledging the posts of others in your network.

You can start the ball rolling by identifying the good prospects that are right under your nose. Look at your network (or have your marketing team look), and identify some likely target companies where multiple people in your firm have a shared connection. You can also see what companies are connected to your own network and create a few pursuits to take advantage of the shared connections. Your leadership will set the tone for everyone else.

GET OFF OF THAT DINOSAUR!

These tips will help you get out of The Stone Age and into The Digital Age:

- Make sure your LinkedIn profile is up to date and interesting.

- Spend three minutes each day looking at what your LinkedIn network is publishing, and like it.

- Track how many visitors to your website come from LinkedIn.

- Invest in software to create one-click publishing for firm-produced thought leadership.

15

What's Next on the Digital Horizon?

At Plante Moran, everyone had annual goals to hit as a way to make sure we were moving the business forward. These goals weren't based on doing our daily jobs but rather things that moved the needle toward future growth.

One year, I came up with what I thought was a genius, albeit a bit evil, idea: I asked everyone on the marketing team to write a 1,000-word-or-less essay on improvements marketing and the firm could make to win more business. Everyone who took this exercise seriously automatically received a "goal" bonus, and the 10 top ideas received "above goal" or "highest level" bonuses.

It was a great exercise in creativity, and it generated a lot of ideas to consider. One that stuck with me was taking a deeper look at companies that were tied to proposal efforts that we'd lost. In some cases, we leveraged the relationships we built in the pursuit to keep the relationship alive, but in many we did not. The idea was simple: give every lost opportunity to a business developer to continue the relationship until the next time we had an opportunity to propose. That winning idea has become a regular part of our pursuit process.

We have a very similar opportunity in our digital world. Whether you're just acknowledging these digital capabilities, already implementing digital tools, or truly leveraging them to benefit your marketing and business development, those tools likely aren't functioning at 100%. There's always room to grow, so let's take a look into the future and ask, "What's next?"

Steve Jobs once said, "A lot of times, people don't know what they want until you show it to them." In this case, comparing where you are today versus what's possible can help you plan for tomorrow.

Here's a summary of where I'd like the firms reading this to be at this point — or at least aspiring toward:

- You're collecting tons of data about the people who interact with your content, including their business category and size.

- You can segment your visitors between ideal prospect, current client, and unqualified buyer.

- You know the kind of content that interests clients and prospects.

- You can see patterns and track how your content needs to evolve across the buyer's journey.

- You can build patterns to show a progression of future business issues that you may want to tackle.

This is a solid start. Through the development of your digital relationships, you know a lot about potential buyers through the data you've collected. But the relationships are more transactional, and the focus more short term. So what does the future hold? Two words: artificial intelligence (AI).

In the digital marketing of the future, your data scientist will lead you on a journey that goes way beyond focusing on the short term that gives more weight to the value of a known qualified buyer and extends your digital relationship more aggressively with the hopes of a future client conversion.

Remarkably, this is similar to the idea of extending the relationship established in a pursuit beyond the bad news that we didn't win the proposal. The end of that purchasing decision refocuses our efforts to areas where we can reasonably obtain future business.

Using AI, you 'll discover patterns that allow you to reasonably predict where your prospects' attention will shift next, giving you the opportunity to try and align your firm with their journey. AI will be key to achieving this next step as it helps you to take a long-term view, segment your data, and get more predictive, but when you achieve success, you'll be able to offer a personalized experience to your buyer's journey and get you closer to winning new work.

Here's a personal example that relates to this issue. Last year I bought a crockpot because I wanted to learn how to make soup. After researching the options, brands, and retailers, I finally settled on my choice. But because the retailers didn't get that memo, they continued to market crockpots to me. No one had an AI tool that said, "He probably bought a crockpot by now; what else can we market to someone who has a new crockpot? A crockpot cookbook? Some crockpot utensils? A crockpot cover? Maybe prepared meals?" Because they lacked that intelligence, they missed the boat.

Business is much the same. Let's say someone is on your website investigating topics related to business succession planning. What might be next up on their journey? And how do your services relate?

Keep the future in mind as you think about your digital tools and your team. Stay on top of how AI will influence professional services marketing. Today, Watson's price point doesn't make it a viable option for most of us, but like all technology, the prices will come down, and options will increase.

Regardless of what the next software will be, success won't be possible without the right team members to bring it to reality. As we said earlier, your marketing team will evolve to include a digital scientist and others who have the training and time to use these new tools to their fullest. They must be comfortable in the world of trial and error. They must be willing to make progress one inch at a time and not be afraid to take little successes and create a new path. This marketing specialty will soon influence almost all of what you do and will be crucial to getting your team to "predict the future" with accuracy.

Another lesson I learned the hard way — and something you can avoid — is that even when your team members have training to use your new digital tools, it won't mean much if they don't have the time necessary to take full advantage of the capabilities. Often, people already have full-time jobs and, despite being eager to help, there isn't time in their day to use the tools. Emails have to be sent, proposals have to be developed, and web content needs to be posted, all of which are important, too. When I was in this situation, I misjudged the time available for my team to embrace new tools. It became my responsibility to make sure to change the schedules of affected team members when we added functionality so we could take full advantage of the new features in our toolbox.

Summary

Self-driving cars may indeed be in our future, but they won't happen without the focus of a whole lot of people in the autonomous vehicle infrastructure. We don't even know about all the roadblocks yet, because some won't even materialize until other problems are solved. Further, self-driving doesn't mean that there won't be an army of people to support the safe use of these autonomous vehicles.

Like self-driving vehicles, many of us see a future where automation will deliver more leads to us than we've ever seen before. But while the future is certain, the path is not. In the future, you want your data to create more of a competitive advantage for your firm in the fight for new clients. However, you don't have to wait for new capabilities to see how it might work. I determined our first scoring model in an Excel spreadsheet with some CRM data and assumptions. If you have an idea, try and model it now, and look for a partner to help you realize your vision. This way, when the future comes, you'll be ready.

GET OFF OF THAT DINOSAUR!

These tips will help you get out of The Stone Age and into The Digital Age:

- Make innovation a part of everyone's job — especially marketing.

- Set specific goals, and reward innovative ideas.

- Consider AI and how you can use it to leapfrog your competition and stay one step ahead in the buyer's journey.

- As you adopt new tools, make sure your team has the time to use them effectively.

Section Four:
It's Hard to Call Your Baby Ugly

Everyone I know loved the show "Mad Men", perhaps because it harkens back to a different time. Life seemed simpler — heck it must have been if you could have a two-martini lunch and still be a wild success (ha-ha) — and until the last 15 years or so, the typical marketing efforts were closely aligned with what we saw in the show.

However, starting in 2007, things began to change at a faster and faster pace, creating an ever-expanding divide between "winners" and "losers." Some of the traditional tactics are largely extinct, like the Yellow Pages, and others have significantly changed. As leaders, we know that many of those entrenched in the old-line marketing tactics haven't generally admitted defeat, but it's our job to determine if and how these tactics play into our digital marketing ecosystem. In the next several chapters, we'll discuss some of the challenges and opportunities facing professional services, wealth management, and not-for-profit organizations today.

16

Ads in Print Publications: Dead or Alive?

It's probably rare that a week goes by when you, or your partners, aren't solicited to buy an ad in a print publication, whether it's a business journal, country club member roster, or local newspaper. These paper-based publications certainly can bring back memories of prestige and importance from days gone by, but that's all changed. The time has passed for the annual Book of Lists that was kept on a shelf and used for reference multiple times per year. Ads in print publications of all types are obsolete. Today people google the information when they need it. And guess what? Your ads are nowhere to be seen.

Despite their near-death status, these publications continue to try to sell ads. It's up to you to raise your defenses and be smarter about taking the bait. When you truly consider the persona of your target buyer, it becomes clear that ads play a tiny, if any, role in their buying decision. Published thought leadership has an impact; pure ads, not so much.

Not all that long ago, we were taught that advertising made the phone ring. While an ad for a good sale (with a coupon!) might attract buyers for consumer products today, you don't often see an ad for a BOGO (Buy One Get One Free) sale for consulting services in your daily newspaper. These print ads worked for consumer goods because sellers invested big time to buy enough ads to achieve the high level of frequency and reach that they needed to invade the subconscious of their audience. How many billions were spent to make "Just do it" roll off our tongues so easily? Many.

This is a high hurdle for professional service firms. Think about the effort (time and dollars) it would require from your marketing firm. Your investment would be used to create the ads in multiple formats for a digital, radio, and print campaign and then you'd need a significant budget to place those ads in the targeted media. If you're like me, you want to spend $50,000 and get the impact of a $1 million campaign. Despite many attempts, I learned the hard way — it doesn't happen.

The Decline of Print Advertising

Estimated print advertising revenue in the United States

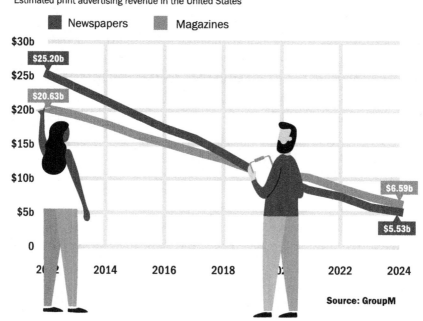

Source: GroupM

There's danger in advertising FOMO (Fear of missing out)

Does the death of advertising seem obvious to you? Good! But your competitors may not be as astute and may still be buying ads. Not so good.

Who among us doesn't have a heightened awareness about our competitors' advertising? When we see them advertise, our logic may disappear, allowing our competitive spirit to take over. We can't let them get head of us! Maybe we should advertise, too!

But the fact is, we (their competitors) are the only ones noticing. Their target audience is largely oblivious. The harsh truth is that if we follow suit and advertise without an integrated campaign, we, too, will have ads that don't drive results — ads that only resonate with our competitors. And the cycle of failure continues.

Executing a pure advertising plan to drive buyer change is a high bar that requires lots of cash. I would encourage most firms to resist the urge for copycat advertising. Focus instead on an integrated approach that incorporates digital outreach, telemarketing, and specifically targeted online advertising that will be more cost-effective per lead.

When I joined Plante Moran, the firm had just launched a test radio advertising program in one market. I wasn't all that keen on the strategy and initially defunded it, but as I started to create my roadmap, I realized that the radio program introduced the Plante Moran brand to audiences who may not be aware of our firm or that we provide services beyond audit and tax. I found that the exposure could reinforce our brand to people who'd seen a piece of thought leadership and influence them to read more and even subscribe. We eventually expanded the strategy to all of our markets, but as digital advertising expanded and as the commercial radio audience shrank, we began to adjust the spend to optimize our integrated strategy.

Media event sponsorships

Newspapers, business publications, industry magazines, and national magazines are shrinking and dying by the day, which is causing them to get creative about offering other options. Many are moving into the event business and offering sponsorships which, at the right price, can be compelling.

While I don't put a lot of value into the package component — after all, the named sponsor will always get top billing — if the sponsorship offers high visibility in front of the right audience, it can be a great way start to an outreach campaign. If you can get an exclusive category package at around $350–$450 per guest, it's probably equal in value to a self-produced event and should be considered. This may be a good replacement to print advertising.

However, be wary when an opportunity seems too good to be true. If a sponsorship suddenly opens up for an event previously sponsored by one of your competitors or an organization that attracts a similar client profile as yours, consider why they might have pulled out before you decide to jump in. If you decide to proceed and the economics make good sense, set some goals for the event, and commit to a formal evaluation immediately following.

Our experience at Plante Moran was a mixed bag. Sometimes these event sponsorships were great, but sometimes they weren't at all what was promised — failing to bring in the target audience that was promised or failing to deliver the agreed-upon number of audience members and relying on our lists to fill seats. You'll never know for sure before the event, so if you're asked to commit to a multiyear package, create criteria for year one that the publication needs to meet or allow you to opt out of the contract.

If you do agree to an event package, you'll want to guarantee a speaking role. Having the opportunity to welcome the guests while introducing yourself and your firm is a minimum. You'll also want to send at least one email to the attendees after the event. And get enough event tickets to bring team members who will "work the crowd."

It may be a good idea to invite a special prospect or client, but the value you're paying for is getting in front of the new audience. Remember to assign roles for your team who will be attending, including networking and follow-up assignments. The attendees likely won't call you after the event; that ball is in your court. It's best when someone who meets them at the event follows up.

I'll add that you should always ask to be on a panel or be part of the presentation, but that's often difficult because the publication tries to separate sales from editorial to show an appearance of independence. As the business model for newspapers continues to shrink, that separation is shrinking, so keep asking.

Summary

Print advertising harkens back to a powerful, but dying, marketing tactic. Don't be the last one on the print advertising ship. Transitioning to the right event sponsorships that are targeted toward the personas you want to reach should provide a better ROI. Just remember that when a sponsorship opens for an ongoing event, it's generally because the previous sponsor wasn't happy with the results. This may not sway your decision to proceed, but do maintain some professional skepticism to decide if your second-year renewal makes sense.

GET OFF OF THAT DINOSAUR!

These tips will help you get out of The Stone Age and into The Digital Age:

- Newspaper advertising on a standalone basis is probably a waste of money for a professional services firm. If you abandon advertising, how does your firm plan to drive new business and new subscribers?

- When you start having difficulty getting people to attend sponsored events, cut back. Forcing these events may not produce the results you anticipate.

- When digital advertising is offered as part of the sponsor-ship package, set up a special code to track the number of visitors and new subscribers it generates.

- Make sure any digital assets offered as part of the sponsorship link back to your website.

- Within 60 days after the event, determine if it actually produced the number of quality attendees that were promised. Use that to figure out your actual cost per attendee for the event.

17

Association Trade Shows:
The Good and The Bad.

Industry and service-based associations and their related trade shows have become big draws for sellers from all areas of the economy. Most of these aim to be "not-to-be-missed" events designed to be their sector's go-to forum for networking, emerging trends, and the unveiling of emerging technologies. The associations have a huge incentive to offer value to their members because of the profits they stand to make by providing a well-attended event, so for the professional service organization that wants access to their association members, these opportunities are generally pay-to-play.

This hyper-competitive environment means that professional service firms think they must spend significant funds to "have a prime seat at the table." Yet the firm that gets the best opportunities is generally not the one that pays the most: instead, it's the firm with the best strategy and execution. Bottom line: You need to understand how to determine the value of a trade show, identify the best opportunities for your firm, and sharpen your ability to negotiate.

Make no mistake about it—executed well, association trade shows are great investments. A meeting filled with clients and prospects under one roof creates very efficient networking opportunities to connect, get acquainted, and schedule meetings. Team members who attend industry trade shows should have one overarching goal: conduct short meetings with new and existing relationships to open the door for longer meetings after the conference is over. That's where future business opportunities can be discussed.

The three best ways to do this are:

- **Get a speaking opportunity that makes people want to hear more about your point of view.** If you impress them, they'll wait for you after your presentation like fans wait for a star quarterback when they leave the locker room after the game. Talk with them, get a card, and set up a Zoom call as soon as possible to learn about their situation. (If you do speak, be sure to include the presentation within your firm bio and your LinkedIn profile. The speeches you give and the conferences you attend add important credibility to your firm and you, personally.)

- **Before the event starts, set up meetings (15–30 minutes) with people you know are attending** to learn what challenges they're working on and/or give them an update on your business. Then plan to talk after the conference. If you've decided to have a booth, it can serve as the rendezvous spot, or you can rent a conference room to hold the meetings.

- **Host a dinner or cocktail reception for several clients and prospects during the conference.** This gives you facetime and a reason to talk after the event. (Consider having a photographer on hand who'll take a picture of the group and send it to your guests when they get home in a frame with your company logo).

In addition to these options, if you're a good networker and are unafraid to start a conversation with people you don't know, introduce yourself to as many people as possible. You have the same goal as above: get agreement to meet after.

Pros and cons of the trade show booth

You may have picked up on the fact that I haven't said you should get a trade show booth. Adopting a trade show practice that points exclusively to a trade show booth is probably the worst investment a firm can make. Why? There are a number of reasons.

First, you're held captive at the booth, keeping you from attending sessions or networking in other places where people congregate during the show.

Second, people manning the booth can't really engage in a conversation because there are so many distractions. Team members tend to be indiscriminate about who they chat with, and good prospects are often overlooked because time is being wasted on the wrong people.

Third, most people aren't trained on how to work a trade show booth. You might think it's a great idea to host games — like a putting green — designed to draw a crowd, but once again, it's untargeted and indiscriminate. If you do get a target, it's a coincidence.

Fourth, trade show booths require a number of professionals to staff it, which drives up your cost and drives down billable time back at the office.

Finally, they're expensive. Generally, when people think about budgeting for trade show booths, they only focus on the out-of-pocket costs, which fail to capture the costs for staff to attend, travel time, booth design, set-up, and promotional items.

For sure, there will be times when a booth is necessary, but before you commit to one, make sure you capture the full cost and ensure you're getting the ROI you want. I've found that a booth is often the first type of sponsorship presented by the industry/service association running the show. If you're considering a new event and you believe the meeting attracts the right audience, why not just start with attendance and networking? And don't fall into the trap of sponsoring a trade show booth in order to evaluate how worthwhile a show is for future attendance. A better way to gauge that is simply to attend, walk around, and interact with other attendees and booth sponsors.

Let's get digital: The rise of geofencing

Some firms are also beginning to add a digital component to conferences, beyond having subscription signups at their booths. One of these tactics is geofencing, an advertising approach that allows you to offer digital ads to people in a certain area. What does that mean?

When people attending a conference use the internet browser on their phone or GPS-enabled computer device (like an iPad), geofencing delivers your ad when they browse. For instance, an attendee may be looking for an article on the top restaurants in Atlanta. If the publisher sells digital advertising space, you could present content as they're looking for a place to eat. Suppose your digital ad offers a popular white paper to conference attendees at the convention center and surrounding hotels for the three days of the conference. This could offer a digital experience similar to, but perhaps more concentrated than, a booth experience.

Summary

Conferences that attract large numbers of your target clients can be great opportunities, but you need to make the economics work for you. Be sure to prioritize speaking opportunities and deprioritize the dreaded trade show booth. When you're buying a package, negotiate for what works for your firm. Sponsors are open to custom designing a package, but you need to ask. Another idea: See if you can join the planning committee, and create an opportunity to showcase your firm's expertise.

GET OFF OF THAT DINOSAUR!

These tips will help you get out of The Stone Age and into The Digital Age:

- Speaking opportunities are one of the best ways for your firm to connect with good prospects quickly. Even if you have to pay or sponsor a show to get the opportunity, it may be worth it.

- Just because a trade show booth is offered as part of a sponsorship package doesn't mean you have to take it. Perhaps you can negotiate for more tickets or just make it a self-serve booth.

- If it makes sense for a multi-day event, give geofencing a try (this option doesn't make sense for a one-day event).

- Force the discipline necessary to evaluate the full investment after each event. Was it worth it for the business generated? (Remember, the onus of this is on the team who attended; the event organizer isn't going to say, "It doesn't look like you got the ROI we talked about." Instead, they'll try to talk you into a bigger booth next year.)

- Promote speeches and conference participation on your website and in proposal documents.

18

Public Relations: Is it Dead Yet?

Have you ever wondered, what will happen to nonprofit organizations whose sole purpose is to raise funds for researching a disease once a cure is found? The logical answer is that they'll declare victory and close up shop, but my bet is that won't happen. My guess is that the organization will shift gears and focus on a different cause where their management believes fundraising has been ineffective or underrepresented.

You can make a similar analogy with public relations (PR). As self-publishing has grown and news outlets have shrunk, the impact of traditional PR has changed. What's left of this dying profession is significantly diluted and often different. You may find this to be a contrarian position, but a lot of people who work in the PR industry want to perpetuate the benefits of this medium. Many marketers got their start in PR, and it's hard for them to concede that it may be going the way of the dinosaurs. In this chapter, I want to make sure your eyes are wide open on how to use public relations today as part of an integrated campaign.

As you think about PR, it's important to separate its effect on you as an individual versus its impact on you as a firm leader and its ability to impact the business decisions you make. They aren't the same.

PR can still influence purchases we make as consumers. For example, you might take action based on a PR tactic that notifies local television stations about an upcoming event. After seeing the news story, you may plan to attend. However, if you read a story in the Wall Street Journal that quotes five different investment advisors on the economy, are you going to pick up the phone and call them? No, you're not! Are you going to even remember their name in 10 days? Probably not.

In a different scenario, imagine you're reading an article that applies to your business in an industry newsletter. Are you going to pick up the phone and call the author? Most likely, no. PR specialists will try to convince you that you will, but ask yourself: when was the last time you were motivated in this way? If you're like me, the answer is never. And if you're in a B2B setting, chances are good that PR alone won't make the phone ring in a significant way, regardless of how prestigious the venue or how much you want it to work.

While there is a place for some PR tactics in your marketing strategy, the typical monthly pricing model to retain a PR firm isn't worth it based on the new business generated. Monthly retainers usually start in the $3,000–$5,000 range. There are very few "must read" publications anymore, so there's more competition for a shrinking number of press outlets. Editors are generally sensitive about mentioning any expert too often, so even when good content is being pitched, barriers are imposed. You might say this seems plausible in cities like Detroit or Cleveland, but certainly not a major city like Chicago. Wrong. In cities like Chicago, the retainers are bigger, and the hurdles greater.

One bright spot with this shrinking industry is that, as staff are cut, prepackaged stories will have an appeal for newspapers and magazines. This may increase your placement options, but you'll still need to carefully customize the mix and price that works for your business.

These prepackaged opportunities are just starting and not the predominant option, but they could be a bright spot in the future.

We've been talking about public relations that focuses on proactive media placement, but here's another form of PR that may come across your desk: Someone representing a national personality contacts your firm and, after citing your expert reputation, they offer you a guest spot in an upcoming production. As you investigate, you realize that they're "pay-to-play." My recommendation is to stay away. They're looking for sponsorship dollars, and the deal will be structured in their best interest, not yours. I found that these requests often come through a partner who's flattered by the invitation and argues that the firm should support them by paying the fee. We were 100% successful in declining these "opportunities," but at times it was hard to get the good of the firm ahead of these egos.

We've talked about the pitfalls of PR, but does it have a solid place in a good marketing strategy? The answer is yes! It has a role when it's part of an integrated strategy and the cost to execute can be justified. PR alone is not enough. Many partners and marketers are "high fiving" themselves when they get a placement, not realizing that the work has just begun. Without a broader plan, the stand-alone media placement will simply be an ego play and worthless to the firm's ability to attract new business.

So, what should you expect from your marketing team when PR is part of the marketing mix? First, you need to identify your goals for the PR tactic. What do you want PR to contribute? Are you trying to burnish your firm's credentials by being published in a credible publication? If so, creating a one-year plan focused on getting published frequently and then developing a marketing piece that highlights your credibility by citing all the places you've been published would be an achievable target. In this case, you could hire a PR firm or even consider doing it yourself with PR software that's available.

Creating this annual summary is priceless content for proposals and websites that's often overlooked by professional service firms. But by creating these summaries, you're adding a powerful message to your audience: "We have recognized thought leaders who work here; if you hire us, you have access to these same experts."

Each of your published pieces can be the centerpiece of a mini campaign. Couple this PR with other tactics such as:

- Posting to the LinkedIn profile of the person quoted.

- Posting to your firm's LinkedIn page.

- Emailing a link to clients and prospects offering to discuss the article's findings. (If you're using a scoring model as we discussed earlier and they engage, it may trigger an action.)

- Posting to your website in the appropriate section.

- Sending to the appropriate referral sources.

Each of these activities is designed to activate the piece and give it more impact. Even if someone doesn't want a meeting after receiving your email, it may be the impetus to get them to subscribe to your newsletter.

After a year, you can evaluate your investment by asking:

- Did the PR effort generate any appointments?

- Did it generate current leads?

- Did it bring you new subscribers?

- Did it add to the firm's brand recognition as experts?

Something outside the box

While traditional PR activities have changed, PR firms are changing, too. At Plante Moran, we used a couple of them in unique ways. In one case, we used a well-connected PR firm in Indiana to help us move into a new market. The PR firm's owner had enjoyed a successful business career in our target area for years, so we selected 20 businesses where he had a personal relationship, and he wrote a letter introducing our firm to these business owners. In another example, we used a PR firm to help us coordinate in-person events in a city where we didn't have an office or staff. Lastly, we used a

PR person to establish a community room — a resource for area nonprofits to hold meetings.

Summary

Public relations is becoming less effective by the day, but it can be useful if it's part of an integrated campaign. A major caveat is to be cautious of the investment and make sure that you can expect an ROI.

It's worth noting that many PR firms have begun to offer other marketing services. They may be an option to provide turnkey marketing help when you're launching new campaigns in conjunction with your PR efforts.

 # GET OFF OF THAT DINOSAUR!

These tips will help you get out of The Stone Age and into The Digital Age:

- Each month, track how many new subscribers came in from PR placements.

- Make sure that you're executing the appropriate follow-up marketing tactics for PR placements.

- Every six months, take a year-to-date look at the benefit of PR to your firm, and consider if a PR firm or a self-publication model is right for you.

- Be on the lookout for ego plays; they generally aren't a good investment.

19

Philanthropy: Is It Marketing?

Charitable giving can present a number of dilemmas to a professional services organization, especially when deserving, respected, or high-profile nonprofit organizations approach your firm. I'll state my point of view on this topic right upfront: You shouldn't intertwine budgets for advertising, business development, and philanthropy, nor should you believe that charitable giving is a means to open doors for new business. (When was the last time you purchased something substantial because the company donated to a charity you support?)

As individuals, it's natural to support the causes you hold dear. It's also important for your firm to participate in philanthropy — but it should be justified based on the cause, its alignment with your firm's interests and values, and the peripheral benefits the support provides to your firm. Creating a budget for your firm's charitable spend is a sound practice, and the program should be measured, celebrated, and potentially even shared with prospects, staff, and recruits.

Create charitable giving guidelines

If you're like me, then you're bombarded with requests for donations from a variety of organizations. It may be hard to say "no" to some, but you can't say "yes" to everyone either, so the more transparent you are, the better.

I recommend that you create guidelines with defined categories, criteria, and a process to respond to the myriad of requests. I recommend transparency. When someone asks for a donation, share the categories where you donate, the criteria you use to make decisions, and when they can expect a decision. This simple process takes a lot of anxiety out of replying to requests. Many requesters will simply go away because they want a donation immediately, they see that they won't quality, or they don't want to put in the effort needed. In each case, they'll feel that they are part of a fair process.

An exception to the rule: Nonprofit sponsorships

Maintaining separate budget buckets for philanthropy, marketing, and business development is a great general rule, but like all rules, there can be exceptions. There may be situations when philanthropy, marketing, and business development merge into one decision point.

Say your firm buys a sponsorship from a nonprofit because their target audience overlaps with your own clients and prospects. The sponsorship may offer some unique and valuable benefits, including event tickets, advertising, speaking opportunities, introductions, or access to their other donors. If the charity audience is your target audience, the donation may qualify as a marketing expense — if it provides the additional coverage you need for this demographic. (The key elements are matching demographics and needed cover- age. If you have matching demographics, but you have already paid for adequate coverage, this will result in a diminishing return.)

If you want to go down this path, don't create an island. The event shouldn't stand alone as a touchpoint. What other marketing efforts can you tie to the event? Will you get email addresses of the attendees so you can correspond with them? Can you invite them to an educational session? Can you offer a free consultation?

Whatever you devise, can you hold yourselves to five new appointments after the event and activities to consider it a success? Can the charity introduce you to decision-makers at your target companies? I think for the three areas (marketing, business development, and philanthropy) to intersect, there needs to be an intentional effort on your part and the charity, otherwise it's still just a donation.

Just be honest with yourself and don't include a donation in your marketing and business development spend when you're holding the marketing team to an ROI.

Board participation and volunteering

Many of your partners and staff volunteer on community and professional boards. This is one subset of charitable spending that you should track for business development efforts. If there's an active member in your firm who's networking and meeting decision-makers on your behalf, you should support them and buy tickets and sponsorships. These investments of time should be tracked in CRM and the cash outlay recorded in its own budget line. If you decide to produce a "state of the firm" annual report in the future, data points like this will be valuable information to include. With CRM, you can also track new business opportunities that result from these relationships.

Often firms will survey their staff and partners to create a central database of their volunteer activities. This information can be useful in pursuits, especially when it identifies nonprofit board members who are potential decision-makers. Does this mapping belong in marketing? Marketing may help with research, the survey, and even drafting an annual plan for strategic donations and involvement, but ultimately the leadership team should guide the process and have final oversight to ensure accountability.

I've seen so many organizations increase their involvement with professional organizations like the Association for Corporate Growth or an industry association in order to be closer to decision-makers, but it may leave their organization with a gap in local community organizations. Many firms sidestep the hard decisions by automatically continuing annual donations year over year despite lack of involvement. In many cases, they can't even fill a table for the annual dinner, but they continue to give. This may be the right decision for the firm, but it should be a conscious decision and not one made because of neglect or inattention.

Client requests

There may be instances when a client requests a donation to their favorite charity. They may tie this request, subtly or overtly, to the potential for ongoing work. In most cases, I've seen, the requests have been modest, but when they weren't, they came from an individual with a large ego who presented other challenges to the client relationship.

If a client asks for a donation, evaluate that request, and make a sound business decision. Is it a cost of doing business with the client and something you wouldn't do if they weren't a client? Is the donation reasonable in relation to the margin you make from their business? It's obviously not a good business choice to donate $10,000 to a client's cause when you only bill that client $20,000. Is it consistent with donations you make for clients of a similar size? This kind of analysis can add clarity and consistency to the process.

Nonprofits as clients

What about professional work you do for nonprofit organizations? It's not uncommon to give nonprofits a discount — many firms follow that practice. Sometimes they work on a fixed fee basis, which is calculated at a reduced billing rate. But if you incur more time than anticipated, there's no remedy to go back to the client for an adjustment, which reduces the billable rate per hour even more.

If you're expected to buy tickets or support the organization in other ways, you can easily find yourself underwater on direct salary costs without any contribution to overhead. This may be consistent with your philanthropic investment philosophy, but you should review these commitments annually to renew your level of support or, if necessary, make changes. If you continue, make sure to count this toward your philanthropic activities.

After reading this chapter, you may be motivated to take a closer look at philanthropy versus marketing. You may even become more strategic about your firm's philanthropy, which could lead to a decision to reduce or eliminate your giving in certain areas. If that's the case, I encourage you to proceed with caution.

These decisions may be startling to the organizations — akin to raising your rates when you haven't done so for years. If you identify organizations where you want to reduce your contribution, you may want to try the following:

- Make a list.
- Create criteria that align with your business.
- Talk to the organizations about how they help your business.
- Create a three-year plan to meet your new goals to avoid any sudden withdrawal or negative effects on the organization.
- Review the list with your partners so everyone is on the same page. It may also give partners an opportunity to increase their personal giving to causes they support.

Summary

Philanthropy is a great investment in your community and can contribute to your firm's reputation. More often than not, it's not marketing and probably doesn't help directly with new business development.

If growing your firm is a goal, don't get sidetracked by mixing the two and thinking philanthropy will play a direct role. Focus on creating an appropriate plan to address growth in addition to your philanthropic activities.

GET OFF OF THAT DINOSAUR!

These questions will help you get out of The Stone Age and into The Digital Age. Ask yourself:

- Has your management team articulated your donation strategy, shared it with marketing, and asked them for a plan that supports it?

- Do you have a database that shows where your partners and staff are volunteering their time? Are most of the important places in your community and professional associations covered?

- Is your firm creating custom ads when there's an opportunity to advertise?

20

A Goal Without a Plan is Just a Wish.

Antoine de Saint-Exupéry once said, "A goal without a plan is just a wish." That might sum up the frustrations that leaders feel when they look back at their growth results over the last 12 months and realize time got away from them — or that their plans weren't concrete or measurable enough.

When you're a leader, you want plans that are a stretch and show real progress; when you're executing those plans, however, you usually want some wiggle room. These contrasting opinions can sometimes result in kicking the annual plan down the road and, before you know it, time has passed without one. However, for leaders with marketing function oversight and a commitment to growth, an annual marketing plan is essential, and you need to find a way to bring all the parties to the table and agree on tactics, timeline, goals, and measurements. It takes discipline, but it's well worth the time.

We've all heard the old adage that says, "When you fail to plan, you plan to fail." I'll add to that, when you neglect to plan, you forgo the benefits of planning, some of which may not be readily apparent. An annual marketing plan gives you the reins to establish priorities and see them through. With a plan, you can better defend against random requests that may come up.

A marketing plan places firm leadership and the marketing team on the same page. You have the opportunity to look forward and review goals, add new goals, and edit priorities, all in a transparent fashion. It can help to calibrate your organization and will inform strategies, tactics, resource requirements, and timelines. Planning presents a great opportunity to review progress and decide whether to continue current efforts or course correct. Always take a look at recurring items with a critical eye. With all the change in our firm's marketing technology, goals, and audience, I found the effectiveness of some tactics can run their course and their ROI can diminish. The annual plan is the perfect time to try something new.

Surprisingly, I found the process helped me get budget increases when we agreed to the tactics upfront. In a few cases, we might have scaled back our plan slightly until the year started to take shape, but our plan had set the table for the next 12 months.

Marketing plan to-dos

At least 90 days before the beginning of the new business year, you should ask your marketing lead to prepare the following:

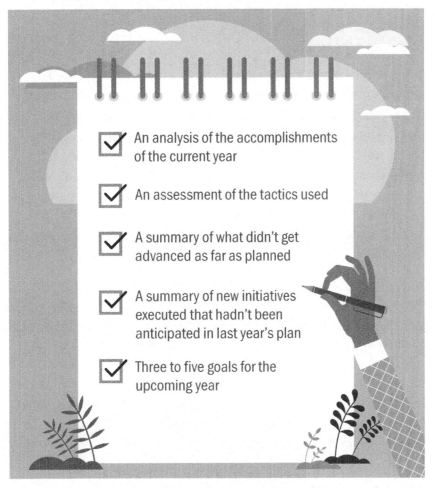

- ✓ An analysis of the accomplishments of the current year
- ✓ An assessment of the tactics used
- ✓ A summary of what didn't get advanced as far as planned
- ✓ A summary of new initiatives executed that hadn't been anticipated in last year's plan
- ✓ Three to five goals for the upcoming year

In building the marketing plan, I suggest everyone agrees on:

- A manageable set of goals that you want marketing to support.
- Detailed tactics for new goals.
- Carry-forward initiatives that didn't get completed.
- A calendarized timeline.
- A budget.

Challenge your marketing team to outline the tactical plans that support each goal. Your plan should include a review of changes in your competitor strategies as well as new business opportunities the firm wants to advance. Again, full participation by marketing, the management team, and client servers will provide the best opportunity for success.

In the annual plans that I created, I took care to articulate the link between marketing's goals and tactics and revenue growth. I tried to be a good steward of the partners' profits and recommended investments that would have a positive impact on growth. In some cases, the tactics had an immediate impact. In others, the goals were achieved over several years through annual tactics that built on one another. This was usually the case when deploying new technology tools. It often took a year to get the core software up and running, another year to complete training and adoption, with full usage in the third.

This was the case when we implemented AI software to automate our lead nurturing program. The software implementation was completed in year one, and the tool began collecting data to customize our approach. When planning for year two, the goal was to fully learn the options the system provided and work for maximum optimization. When year three arrived, we planned for full utilization of the tool. The marketing plan for each year looked ahead to the full benefit and described the incremental benefits we were making along the way.

Strive for multifaceted marketing plans

One of the key takeaways of this book is that standalone tactics are rarely successful. A well-developed marketing plan combines complementary tactics to get the best results. I'm wary of any marketing plan with just one tactic for each goal, as a single tactic plan tends to produce underwhelming results.

So what does a good, multifaceted plan look like? Consider these tactics designed to generate more wealth management leads:

- Digital advertising campaign to capture new audiences
- Thought leadership piece(s) to impress the reader
- Subscription offer
- Refer-a-friend campaign
- Radio campaign
- Event sponsorship
- PR initiative intended to bring financial literacy education to urban high school youth

An integrated campaign to achieve more tax revenue might include:

- Speaking opportunity at a conference
- Geofencing conference attendees
- Thought leadership piece
- Internet advertising
- Telemarketing campaign
- Free, 30-minute consultation offer

Each of these tactics is timed and layered to complement the others and must include some time for an appointment-setting component. For example, if you had the opportunity to speak at a conference, but you didn't follow up with conference attendees, the opportunity would not be fully optimized.

By creating a marketing plan, you set your intentions and a course of action. Sharing the plan at a high level with the firm will give everyone a greater insight. As additional marketing requests come up during the year, you'll have a framework to evaluate them and to green-light them, or not.

Remember, when new things do come up, you can't just keep piling on your marketing team and expect them to absorb the added workload. The strain could affect quality, turnover, or morale, so you need to be prepared to either renegotiate the plan or find a way to fund additional capacity. Reviewing your marketing plan quarterly allows you to monitor progress, and it gives you an opening to discuss with your marketing lead what options you have if tactics from your original plan are derailed or if you want to accelerate your growth plans.

Lastly, make your marketing investment count. Go big or go home: I worked hard to avoid numerous small investments which appeased my internal clients, but were too small to have any impact. Another area where being intentional can make a huge impact.

Wrapping up the year

As you end the budget year and start the next, it's a good time to pause and reflect about how the marketing lead has contribut- ed to your firm's growth. At this point, you may also want to seek feedback from your partners about what they think went well with marketing and what might be improved. With your results and your partners' input, you can have a very transparent conversation with your marketing lead about strengths and opportunities for improve- ment. You may find that new resources are needed to support added volume or to add a broader set of skills. In some cases, you may have been relying on outside consultants to augment your marketing team and now the volume is sustained at such a level that you've surpassed the "breakeven" point to hire the resource directly. These healthy conversations support your goals, develop your staff, and avoid unnecessary turnover.

During my time at Plante Moran, I was glad that the process was so transparent, even though at times it made me uncomfortable. I remember one meeting in a room with several growth leaders where I'd requested more marketing team members; before approving my request, the room was offered the opportunity to comment. In other firms, this may have taken place with me standing in the hallway, but not at Plante Moran. Despite me being in the room, everyone was open and honest. I got a lot of support, but I also learned who I wasn't supporting as much as they'd like. I was uncomfortable, but it was a very healthy experience and a good reminder about how partnerships are different from corporations.

From those conversations, I learned quickly that everyone's needs must be addressed at some point. You can only deprioritize a partner's needs for so long before other partners begin to add their voice to the neglected partner's request and the overall sentiment begins to affect how the partners collectively feel about marketing's performance.

Although it was challenging, I needed to find a way to assist even the smallest practices every 24 months. All partners have growth goals and need help. If resources aren't available — and additional resources aren't an option — this should be addressed with the requesting partner by the managing partner and the head of marketing. This way, that lack of support won't be viewed as solely a marketing decision.

Summary

The marketing plan helps to actualize your growth plans by articulating the objectives, tactics, and timeline and establishes a benchmark to measure progress. As we said earlier, no one is perfect. We all have our strengths and weaknesses. As a leader overseeing marketing, your job is to understand both strengths and weaknesses of your CMO and have a plan to leverage their strengths and to help offset their weaknesses. This could involve training, hiring a team member with complementary skills, or outside consultants. The annual review of accomplishments and goal-setting can be the difference between a CMO that lasts two years and one that lasts 10 years. I don't have to tell you: your ROI is improved with a successful CMO who stays for the long term.

GET OFF OF THAT DINOSAUR!

These tips will help you get out of The Stone Age and into The Digital Age. Ask yourself:

- Make sure you start on your marketing plan 90 days before the new period begins.
- Review goals quarterly.
- Require integrated tactics when possible.

See Tool 11 in the appendix for a sample integrated marketing plan.

21

Your Party, Your Rules.

When you're hosting an event, you have 100% control and responsibility to make sure that your guests fondly remember their time with you. In my professional career, I've been a guest or a host at many outstanding corporate events, and as I look back, there are four or five that still make me smile.

There was a magical, but very loud, afternoon, in the pit at a NASCAR race. A baseball game at Comerica Park where 15 executives entered the suite as strangers and left as friends. A fine dinner with German executives, where I tasted my first (and last!) $200 bottle of wine. And a sales event where my picture was taken with Whoopi Goldberg. Each of these events made a lasting impression.

Hosted events can play an unbelievably valuable role in attracting new clients and showing your gratitude to existing ones. In the past, many firms relied exclusively on entertainment for client appreciation and to woo prospects, but in today's tech-centric and online world, hosted events allow "that something more," a personal touch in a digital conversation that can give an extra boost to your online marketing programs. Worst-case scenario, these events show the companies in your pipeline that you're not taking them for granted. Best case: They put you over the top and seal the deal.

Make a memorable experience

The key to executing an event that complements and advances an opportunity is to make your guests feel special. What makes them feel special? A bespoke opportunity or venue, genuine hospitality expressed in unexpected ways, and wonderful guests who can all contribute to an event that creates a lasting impression.

However, spending alone won't meet your goals. You need a personal touch to curate a special experience. A few firms do this very well. It may be as elaborate as a once-a-year destination conference or as simple as a new feature added to an annual event.

SPORTS ENTERTAINING HAS RISKS AND REWARDS

Professional sports teams have some of the best salespeople I've ever seen. Many of them are exceptional at convincing professional service firms to spend more money on sponsorships and suites than they can ever get back in new business. To convince you to spend, they may even wave the carrot of steering new business from the team your way. But rarely do firms end up with new work from the team or a positive ROI. Why?

Because the sellers are better at selling than firms are at buying. You spend tens of thousands of dollars for curated opportunities that are presented as "game-changers," but what happens? Most tickets don't get used for business development, you don't have a way to track new business from suite entertainment, tickets are given out too late, and invitations go to important clients who are already busy. In short, the investment is poorly managed, and your firm ends up paying for tickets, dinner, and drinks for various staff who may or may not be the top talent you want to retain.

Here are some simple rules to follow when you want to use hosted events as part of a successful prospect recruitment and client appreciation strategy:

- When you have season tickets for sporting events, use software to manage ticket requests that requires information about the business purpose, including whether it's a new business opportunity or for client retention. Preschedule a follow-up meeting with firm partners to discuss next steps that arose during the event.

- Start small. Can you get the suite for six-to-eight games instead of the entire season? If it goes well, expand.

- Appoint someone to manage the ticket distribution, curate the events, and create accountability for ROI.

- Give an appropriate gift to guests to remember the event.

- Make sure unused tickets go to staff who you want to reward.

Here are a few additional points to keep in mind:

- Invitations take time. Your teams should have at least two months before the event date to extend invitations and gather RSVPs.

- Firm-purchased tickets are for the firm. The same rules should apply to everyone who has business development goals. A partner's personal needs shouldn't preempt firm business, no matter where the partner ranks in the firm.

- If you commit to a sponsorship package with media opportunities, consider getting an independent evaluation of the value of the media offered. Chances are it's not as valuable as the value assigned in the package, and you may want to ask them to sweeten the pot to make up the difference.

- If you're negotiating a package, consider asking for an appearance(s) from a team player, alumni, or mascot. That can go a long way to create a unique experience that makes your guests feel special.

- Signed jerseys, balls, and hats can easily be negotiated into packages and will add that extra "special something" to your hosted events.

Other firm-hosting opportunities

Most firms offer webinars as part of their marketing mix, but in-person events allow you to build a personal bond that can help the sales process. In addition to business meals, consider the following:

- Firm-sponsored seminars. These can include everything from a breakfast information session to an all-day event.

- Invite your client(s) to join you at a business luncheon or a note-worthy event hosted by an association or business publication.

- Firm-sponsored fun events. These can include conversations with sports figures, golf practice at the beginning of the season, or batting practice for kids and grandkids.

Whatever you do, think about ways you can add something special. You want your guests to walk away and tell their friends about your event. I had the good fortune to talk with a corporate meeting host who shared a perspective that completely changed my thinking about these events. Her recipe was to always add an unexpected fun component. At one event, she hired a high school marching band to walk through the crowd just as their morning event was kicking off.

At Plante Moran, we took her advice and incorporated her out-of-the-box thinking into a few events. We hosted a business seminar at the symphony and added a drumming lesson before intermission. The energy was electric as we went into a break and a short networking session.

At another event, our attendees made Halloween baskets for children in a local cancer ward. These activities made the events memorable to even the most cynical attendees who may have expected to come to our session, drink coffee, and take in information. Hospitality like this can make your attendees feel special.

If your plans call for out-of-town events — perhaps you're actively courting business in cities where you don't have offices — they can still be memorable, with a little extra effort. I'd recommend hiring a local event company or a "single shingle" PR person to help you plan the event. They'll bring a perspective that you may not have and will give you access to information about unique venues and local preferences that will help you launch your brand. The cost would be minimal and could help you enter a new market with greater confidence.

Plan for follow-up in advance

When hosting events, the follow-up is just as important as the pre-event planning. I suggest that, when scheduling your planning meetings, add a post-event follow-up as well. The follow-up should happen within 48 hours of the event while everything is fresh. The most important topic will be the opportunities discovered during the event. Talk about what was learned, and plan follow-up actions with the appropriate individuals in the firm. For example, one of the attendees may have expressed a concern about cyber-security, but everyone on the host committee was from the tax team. Including a cyber expert in the follow-up will improve the chances to win the business.

It's also important to debrief about each of the guests who attended because, even though there may not be any opportunities with them today, that doesn't mean there might not be opportunities down the road.

One time, the business developer and I were debriefing after hosting a small group in a suite. They were all fantastic people who would be fun to work with, but we couldn't come up with a single opportunity to pursue immediately. However, within three years we'd obtained work with half of them; it just took a little time for the right opportunity.

As part of your integrated marketing strategy, you should make sure that everyone you hosted is:

- Connected to all the event hosts on LinkedIn.
- Subscribed to your thought leadership programs.

Finally, when there are "in-person events," it's a nice touch to have a photographer on hand. That way you can follow-up with your guests and give them a group photograph in a nice, firm-branded frame — it's a great way to get back in front of the prospect after the event and to keep you top of mind.

Conclusion

If you're going to include hosted events in your plan, make them special. Events should be attended by lots of people from your firm, probably a three-to-one ratio of guests to firm staff. It doesn't do as much good if your guests can't talk to firm representatives or they don't feel like they were treated like royalty. Events that are generic and on autopilot won't produce a good ROI; put simply, it's not worth doing if you don't do it well, so whatever your budget, make it something special. Lastly, be wary about the great selling skills of professional sports teams. They'll make it seem that using their venue to sell is as easy as falling off a log. It isn't.

GET OFF OF THAT DINOSAUR!

These tips will help you get out of The Stone Age and into The Digital Age:

- Set a 36-month ROI and hold your firm accountable.

- If part of the event spend is for staff reward, set the goal and measure it.

- Make sure you commit to tickets at least two months before the event, so you can get on the calendar of decision-makers who may be in demand.

Section Five:
If It Were Easy, Everyone Would Do It

Connecting the dots to create a healthy and successful business generation machine is complicated — and it's getting harder and harder by the day. Focusing on some of the basics can help.

In this last section, I want to share a few areas that are always worth remembering to make the most of every opportunity.

22

Pipeline Management.

A pipeline is traditionally defined as a group of prospective new clients for your firm. These prospects may range from "cold" to "warm" — companies that you've never had a discussion with to people who've given you an RFP. The pipeline is often depicted as a widemouthed funnel that gets narrower and narrower as the business gets closer to an RFP and becoming a new client.

The pipeline is broken into "categories" to group businesses in similar stages of the buying process. In a traditional sales organization, you might have four to six categories. In a five-category approach, the pipeline begins after the prospect leaves the nurturing phase. At that point the stages are: awaiting the first meeting, ongoing discussions in progress, specific opportunities being discussed, RFP in process, and lastly, the win or loss.

What's pipeline management? And how does it apply to a professional services organization?

In a traditional sales organization, each salesperson's pipeline is vigorously reviewed weekly or monthly to make sure that they're full of vetted, viable prospects. While I was at Nextel, our methodology required the prospect to agree to the next meeting for an opportunity to stay in the pipeline. Why were they so concerned about the quality of the pipeline? Because it was used to make revenue projections, information that was critical for a public company like Nextel that reported earnings quarterly. If the pipeline wasn't projected to reach the desired sales numbers, the company might institute incentives for the customer or the sales team to increase the forecast. Conversely, if sales were running ahead of plan, they could pull those marketing dollars back.

Typical Sales Funnel

The pipeline in a professional services organization is much different. If you're a firm leader, sector leader, or office leader you'll find that creating a pipeline allows you to:

- Monitor efforts to attract "dream clients."

- Predict periods where there will be a drought or even a surplus of work.

- Identify potential new business to replace lost clients.

- Calibrate hiring requirements.

In professional services, the first key is to keep the pipeline simple. I've seen too many people who are new in professional services create models that are too cumbersome for the field. And make sure your pipeline is more than a list of businesses who might be clients if you ever get around to trying to contact them. It should represent organizations where there's a concrete plan of action, meaning someone should be touching them every 3–6 months to maintain a place in your funnel; otherwise, they can go back to a digital nurturing campaign.

Pipeline stages to consider

Most CRM systems have an embedded function that allows you to define the stages in your pipeline and review what's in it. Usually, you can filter the organizations by total firm pipeline, office pipeline, and industry or service line pipeline.

Here are the stages that I recommend, starting at the top of the funnel:

- **Stage 1:** Prospects that have been identified as potential future clients but have not been assigned to anyone to begin working. This might be slightly unusual, but it creates a place to store company names for future follow-up and avoids muddying up other stages.

- **Stage 2:** All first appointments in progress from digital efforts.

- **Stage 3:** Prospects that partners and staff are actively working. (If a Stage 3 prospect goes 90 days without a touchpoint from the pursuit team, it should be disqualified and moved back to a previous stage.)

- **Stage 4:** Organizations that have acknowledged they need your services, and you're working to identify scope, timing, and next steps. To be in this category, the pursuit team must have (a) met with them within the past 90 days and (b) have another action step planned within the next 90 days.

- **Stage 5:** Active proposal or RFP in process.

- **Stage 6:** Won.

- **Stage 7:** Lost, no chance of future business.

- **Stage 8:** Lost, but returned to Stage 3 for ongoing pursuit or digital nurturing with semiannual, personal follow-up.

By creating rules and activities to manage your pipeline, you can begin to create a mathematical relationship between the number of Stage 3 businesses that make it to Stage 4. You can do the same for Stage 4 to 5, and then Stage 5 to 6. By creating and monitoring these numerical relationships, you'll have useful tools to help forecast future business. If you see client assignments ending or the loss of a client, you can use the pipeline to get an idea of what's there to replace it. You can even activate programs to try and accelerate new business if needed. With a fertile pipeline, you may not have all the current business you need, but you'll have a pool of likely possibilities for future work.

Part of the input for Stage 3 should be targeted pursuits — businesses that meet your ideal client profile. Like any "Blue Sky" effort, this can be difficult to narrow down when there aren't clear parameters. You may sometimes pick challenging targets and bypass ones that are more easily won.

I would apply these three filters to identify and qualify your list of targets:

- Using LinkedIn, what businesses in your target revenue size and industry have connections with people working at your firm?

- Using LinkedIn, what businesses in your target revenue size and industry have direct relationships with people in your firm's network (second-degree connections)? Are they strong enough to make an introduction for you?

- What target prospects have one or more firm connections in your firm's CRM system?

By creating your target list with warm contacts, you'll jumpstart your effort and have a greater shot at success. This exercise also ensures that members of your team understand who your ideal prospects are and why — with the ancillary benefit of preventing time wasted on unqualified prospects.

We realize there are many reasons why new business may not advance so neatly and sequentially through your pipeline. Some prospects may skip stages. If your firm has a strong referral network from centers of influence, a lot of prospects may start in Stage 4 and 5. This is all great! It's hard to get new business, and none of it falls off the trees, so this is something to be celebrated.

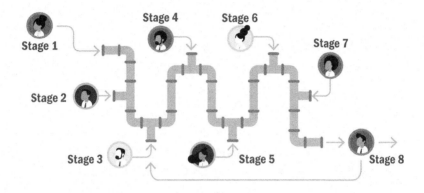

Don't underestimate your role as a leader

As a leader, it's unrealistic for you to be involved in every opportunity, so what's the best way to help? Here are a few best practices:

- Each month, work with your team, and identify two "Stage 4 businesses" where your personal involvement might help move a prospect to Stage 5.

- Create accountability for new business activity — and make sure it's tracked. Too often, more time is spent on identifying the target than on the pursuit. (This is like planning a charity benefit where everyone wants to pick the kind of chicken served for dinner, and no one wants to sell sponsorships and tickets.) You need to create a periodic forum (at least monthly) where each pursuit team discusses their progress. Everyone must talk about what has, or hasn't, happened.

- If teams aren't making progress, determine if you have too many targets — or maybe the wrong team is assigned. Make adjustments as appropriate.

- If activities aren't being completed, try shortening the time between meetings to heighten accountability and keep the process top of mind.

- When people are asked to report activities on a target, don't allow a bait and switch. All too often, I've heard, "We don't have anything to report on ABC company, but let me tell you about XYZ; we're working on a new proposal that came from a referral source." This allows the team to "get off the hook" for not completing their assignment. I suggest you save 15 minutes at the end for people to talk about/brag about new business that came in from other channels.

- Look for skill gaps that you observe through the sales process and provide opportunities for your teams to improve. For instance, say you observe that someone has a lot of first meetings but can't get the same prospect to commit to a second. Address this, and recommend new strategies. Don't wait for a career planning meeting.

Lastly, in today's business world dominated by private equity ownership that buys and sells businesses at speeds rarely seen before, your pipeline can be adversely affected due to a sale that was unanticipated. It's critical to replace work as soon as you know that an organization may leave you; don't wait for the revenue pipeline to come to a halt. This is another great reason why a well-articulated and developed pipeline is critical to today's successful leader.

Summary

With proper insight, you can create and manage a pipeline focused on opportunities that have the greatest potential. Done well, the pipeline can keep everyone focused on where their efforts can do the most good. Through diligent pipeline management, you can help to reduce the amount of time when your team isn't billable. If you're going to start a pipeline for your firm, instead of enlisting the entire team, you may want to start with the practice that has the lowest percentage of billable hours compared to their peers.

GET OFF OF THAT DINOSAUR!

These tips will help you get out of The Stone Age and into The Digital Age:

- Keep the pipeline clean. Set hard rules for what qualifies for each stage; this will give you more actionable data.

- Determine your firm's ratios. Look at the funnel for the last six months:

  » What percentage of proposals did you win?

  » What percentage of proposals started in Stage 4? What percentage in Stage 5?

  » If you want 10% more opportunities in the proposal phase, how many opportunities do you need in Stages 4 and 5?

- Be sure to hold periodic meetings to review the pipeline. While a marketing person or other administrative staff can help to prepare the various analytical points to cover, you need to run it. Don't delegate this important responsibility to anyone with lesser authority. If it's not important enough for you to lead, it won't be perceived as important enough for the partners to comply.

- Keep track of clients who leave your firm. Monitoring what goes out the back door can be more difficult, but it's worth the extra effort to capture this useful data.

- Pipeline management and sales are a study in continuous process improvement. Look for things to reward, emulate, and improve. Keep the dialogue open, and create an environment where everyone wants to do better.

23

Before You Can See
an Opportunity...

Before you can see an opportunity, you have to look for it and, as a growth-minded firm, look no further than your current clients. They provide a wonderful opportunity for you to sell additional services.

Your clients know you and trust you. They believe you provide value for what you bill, and they believe you have their best interests at heart. If they have a business need that you can address, they'll be all too happy to pay you to address it. But are your partners and staff aware of all of the services you offer? (It's a sad day when a colleague refers a good client to another professional because they aren't aware that your firm had the capability to solve the client's problem.)

Knowing your services is only half the battle, however; you also need to know how to identify signs that a client needs additional help. While your seasoned pros likely have all of this covered, what about younger staff — or new staff joining your firm?

They're likely not as knowledgeable — particularly since staff members have different specialties, so they have different lists of "other services" that they typically offer to clients. It's challenging to learn everything. But learn everything, they must. After all, their ability to help grow firm revenues depends on their recall of your firm's offerings, something that may be easier said than done.

When I was a young staff accountant, the number of services my firm offered had just started to grow, and I took the responsibility to stay current on these items very seriously. But at some point, the number of services got so large that it challenged the comprehension and retention of even the most committed staff. Sound like your firm? If so, someone has to help your staff keep up, as the more staff know, the better your chances are that they'll recognize the signs when a client could use one of your services and know who to connect them with to help.

Ask your marketing leader to create a multiyear plan to get the ball rolling. A multiyear plan will emphasize that the need never stops, which is something this knucklehead (your author) didn't initially realize. This is a great opportunity to allow the team to demonstrate their creativity.

As a starting point, I suggest an easy-to-carry booklet that lists all your services and some telltale signs that indicate that a client may have a problem. I'd also emphasize to staff the wonderful resource that your website provides. It's written in basic terms to educate people outside your organization, so it should be a must-read for all staff.

However, that's not enough to reach your goal. Marketing needs to make it fun. Consider producing podcasts or webinars where your team members can explain to their peers what their service offerings are and all the details, they need to identify opportunities — and end those programs with a quiz and prizes. Another idea: deliver content to staff's cellphones queued up so they can get to it at a more convenient time. I suggest you run a program for 6–8 months and then pause and give the audience a small break to refresh before starting a new effort.

These efforts will be most effective when they're combined with reinforcements from the partners and your management team. Are partners asking staff about the offerings that are discussed? Are staff encouraged to participate? Are partners or staff asked to reteach the content presented?

Conclusion

If helping your clients by offering additional services is important to your firm, you need to get your team familiar with your firm's services. Providing job aides that make it easy to diagnose client problem areas and tie them to firm services is key and will be a good support for your client service teams (and free them from relying on their memories). And remember — this is an ongoing process that will never end. To succeed, it will need to be reinforced by firm leadership.

 GET OFF OF THAT DINOSAUR!

These tips will help you get out of The Stone Age and into The Digital Age:

- Track year-over-year growth in revenue to existing clients.
- Track revenue by service to clients that are new to the firm. The reciprocal will show how well you're penetrating your existing clients.

24

The Closest You Get to a New Client — A Proposal.

While it's true that the closest you'll ever be to a new client is during the proposal process, it usually doesn't get the respect it deserves. It's time for some truth-telling about proposals:

- While working on a proposal is typically the last activity before landing a new client, it's probably not consistently your best effort.

- A proposal is often treated as a check-the-box activity. If it gets ignored until the last minute, you run out of time — and you lose the opportunity to make a big impression.

- Many firms complete 90% of a proposal by recycling and updating an old proposal, even though they know that the repurposed proposal doesn't express the custom experience they're promising to deliver.

I recognized early in my time as CMO the importance of having a distinct proposal process and a designated team to coach the partners and produce documents that resonate with potential buyers.

The proposal isn't just a flat documentation of your qualifications; it lays out a valuable opportunity to show your prospects what their experience will be when working with your firm. For those reasons, it's important to gather the right team who'll embrace all aspects of the purchaser's process and produce a document that's written from the buyer's perspective.

This is a great opportunity to gather a team from a variety of backgrounds, including staff who will be on the client service team and members of your marketing and sales teams. The team needs to dissect the proposal request and determine the following:

? **Why is the prospect seeking a new service provider?**

? **What are the decision criteria?**

? **Who are the decision-makers?**

After the team's first collaboration, it's not uncommon for them to come up with a series of unanswered questions that they'd like the prospect to answer so you can give them your best work. The willingness of the lead partners to go back and ask more questions will be a great indicator of the collaborative nature of your team.

Start with low-hanging fruit

While whole books are written about the proposal process, let's take a few minutes to look at low-hanging fruit that will enable you to generate a winning proposal quickly.

First, put the buyer's persona front and center. The team discussion we just talked about is a start, but you need to make sure the proposal document is written from the buyer's perspective; it's not enough to say, "We understand them." You have to write to them.

This is usually harder than you think because the propensity is to write proposals that you want to read, based on the mistaken assumption that you're the same as the decision-maker; you're not. Everyone on the team should have the opportunity to challenge the proposal and whether it meets the needs of the persona. The partners may have the most technical knowledge, but they're not the best people to wordsmith the document. If you want the best proposals, don't let team members' talents get run over. For example, when reviewing suggested edits, don't assume that the edits by the last person trump all others simply because they came in last. The document owner gets to decide which edits are accepted and rejected based on merit alone.

Marketers who have a background in proposals or other elements of the sales process will be your best resources. They understand the process and know how to negotiate with the partners. If marketing or sales doesn't have these qualifications, getting them coaching and helping them develop a process is a great step with a fantastic ROI. Depending on the demand for proposals compared to your other marketing activities, it may be necessary to create a team focused exclusively on generating the best proposals. This will prevent your marketing efforts from being derailed every time you get one.

One helpful exercise I've found is to think about proposals that you've received when you're the buyer. What did they say or do that resonated with you? How does that compare to the proposals your firm is generating? With the software available today and the talent of young marketers, high-quality proposals are within every firm's reach, no matter the budget. Today, it's easier than ever to produce a proposal that incorporates infographics to help tell your story. In my time in the accounting world, a study showed the average business leader spent six minutes reading a proposal, and one of them was the fee page. (If I'm being honest, that's about how much time I spend reading large proposals; how about you?) To combat decreasing attention spans, graphics are gaining ever-increasing value in all communications, and proposals are no exception.

Ideally, a proposal will be the result of a pursuit effort where you already have a personal relationship with the prospect — where it's the natural "next step" in the buying process. Most organizations will have sophisticated purchasing functions, so even if the decision-makers want to give you the work, they may have to go through a bid process. Hopefully it's just a formality to make sure they have a viable solution and to provide a price reference. However, anytime your competitors are introduced into the process, you need to stay on top of your game and maintain close communication with your buyers.

What happens when you receive a request for proposal from an organization where you don't have a relationship with the buyer? You start as the underdog. Before you go through the time-consuming process of generating a proposal, you need to assess the situation. Do you have an ideal solution that, once the prospect gets to know you, will give you a good chance of winning? Then by all means, proceed. However, if after doing your research, it seems the odds are against you (and they usually are if you don't have any contacts at the organization), the smart money is to decline to bid. Often in these situations you're only being asked to propose to provide the comparative price points purchasing needs to sign off on the company they want to award the business to. They usually give you a short deadline, and the request can create a lot of unnecessary turmoil inside your firm.

In select cases, you may decide to play a long game if you don't have a relationship with the company today but view the proposal process as foot in the door. Here you're accepting the probability that you'll lose the first bid in favor of building relationships so that, come the next proposal, you'll have an inside track. This will take effort, including a quarterly touchpoint strategy, but it can pay off with the right targets.

A word to the wise: You may have a relationship with the prospect and not even know that you do. As we've discussed, there are many ways for people to build an appreciation for your firm that's not on your radar. A thorough search of your marketing data is in order if you get a proposal from someone where you're not aware of a relationship. I suggest you at least check the following:

- Have they attended a webinar you hosted?
- Have they subscribed to your newsletter(s)?
- Have they visited your website and downloaded content?
- Are they connected to people at your firm through LinkedIn?
- Did they previously work at a client?
- Has anyone at your firm met with them and recorded a meeting in CRM — whether in their current position or a previous one?

If you find a connection, you've struck gold! Understanding the category of the content the prospect has consumed can give you a leg up on their burning issues. Certainly, knowing who from the prospect used your content is also very valuable.

If you really want to double down on your proposals and establish a proposal support team that can help partners and staff better compete, you need to consider the following elements:

- Invest in proposal software that starts every proposal as a unique project. The number-one mistake made by professional service firms is to use an old proposal as the starting point for a new one. The opportunity to miss some of the new client updates is huge — what happens when search and replace isn't enough?

- Establish guidelines about which proposals qualify for help. If you have a small proposal, perhaps you don't put proposal team resources behind it. Reserve those for the largest and most prestigious proposals.

- Treat each proposal as a project. Good project management skills should prevail.

- One of the biggest hurdles to developing a quality proposal is time. Often, requests for proposals sit on partners' desks for indeterminate amounts of time, which eats into the time needed to work on the proposal. Empower administrative assistants to identify proposals and start the process even before the partner has time to contribute actively.

- As part of your proposal team, establish a knowledgeable project lead who can review the request and determine if it's a likely candidate to pursue. Generally, it will be, and they can review technical requirements like indemnification, start draft language, and suggest a pursuit team.

- Format your proposal so that decision-makers can hit the high-lights in six minutes or less. Make sure they're visually appealing.

- Proposals need to be a combination of words and illustrations. A skilled graphic designer should be part of your proposal team to tailor the message (either on your team or under contract).

- Overviews at the beginning should be just that, overviews. They should say something different than the proposal itself. Consider putting the fee in the introduction, as that's generally the main thing the reader wants to see.

- As often as possible, give the prospective client a draft of the proposal for review and comment before it's issued as final.

- If a partner doesn't want to work collaboratively or take input from others, don't force them to use proposal resources. It will just waste time and create frustration.

- Ask your proposal team members to join APMP (Association of Proposal Management Professionals), and invest in their development as professionals.

Good proposals that best represent your firm and help you win new business are generally a collaborative effort. As you develop your proposal team, I suggest that you first offer the resource to partners who want to work collaboratively. If a partner or pursuit team leader has a "my way or the highway attitude," don't waste the money when a typist will probably do.

At Plante Moran, we started talking about a dedicated proposal team back in 2009. Many of our industry group leaders were concerned that our proposals were too wordy and didn't deliver what prospects wanted. They worried that our proposals weren't competitive. As we discussed options, we were a little surprised when several leaders expressed support for a dedicated proposal team. It started very small and was always an option, not a mandate. The team proved to provide a valuable service, and partners commented on the team's contribution. Due to partner demand, the team has grown to be one of the largest units of the marketing department.

While your firm may not have the luxury of a separate team, a contractor may be a worthwhile addition when bidding on an important new client as we discussed under the hybrid option of staffing marketing efforts.

Summary

A thorough understanding of the RFP is the most critical component of creating an effective proposal. This includes gaining a good understanding of the prospect and their position in the market. Reviewing your digital data to see where prospects have connections with your firm can give you a leg up, as well as understanding LinkedIn connections and other ties.

Tier the level of effort in preparing a proposal to the economic value to your firm. If it's a small project, but a good introduction to a larger client, it may be as important as a large proposal and deserving of a significant investment, as large proposals will probably be infrequent.

 # GET OFF OF THAT DINOSAUR!

These tips will help you get out of The Stone Age and into The Digital Age:

- Invest resources to develop and update proposal templates at least annually.

- Create a graphics library with frequently used pieces.

- Develop proposal performance metrics.

- Develop a matrix to guide the decision of when to respond to proposals with no known connections.

25

Everyone Loves a Story!

For many years, I attended a brunch to support the Michigan Humane Society. One year they opened with a video that told a moving story about an adult dog who was chained up in its owner's backyard when, for no reason, the next-door neighbor poured gasoline on the dog and lit it on fire. The dog suffered severe burns, and the Humane Society came to the rescue by providing help at no charge through their Pet Aid Fund.

The owner eventually surrendered the dog to the Humane Society because they couldn't care for the injured animal. The Humane Society nursed the dog until it was fully recovered and, when it was ready for discharge, they adopted the animal to a child who was recovering from severe burns and had recently been released from a children's hospital.

The video said that all this was possible thanks to people like me who had supported the Michigan Humane Society in years past. To continue this work, they said, everyone had to help. When the lights went up and they asked us to raise our hands if we were willing to donate $500 to continue their pet rescue, hundreds of hands flew up — and there wasn't a dry eye in the house.

The Humane Society could have simply told us about the animal rescue program and given us statistics about how many animals had been saved. They could have shared the number of brave men and women who worked there and the total cost of the program. But they didn't do any of that. They told that story, and it was the most successful fundraising effort I've ever seen!

Storytelling is one of the most powerful techniques we can use to communicate with our audience. It has a place in our content, proposals, and business development interactions because of how it engages people by appealing to their human nature. Storytelling can work no matter who you're trying to engage — prospects, clients, or staff — and it works whether you're writing or speaking. While not all stories can tug at the heart strings like The Humane Society's, they can convey why specific information is important, how it can impact us, and what might happen if we don't heed a warning.

Earlier, we talked about meeting your audience where they are in order to help them move forward. Take, for example, the company who hesitated to invest in an ERP (enterprise resource planning) system because they felt their operation wasn't big enough. They'd been using a manual 3x5 card system, and they felt that was enough to get them by. What if we told them a story about a similar-sized manufacturer that felt the same way?

In our story, this manufacturer saw that their inventory balance and carrying costs were increasing and, upon further inspection, found that their part-forecasting process was out of kilter because of a new hire who wasn't familiar with their manual processes. Several part shortages then led to extra parts being ordered across the board, which increased inventory levels. If there had been an ERP system in place, the company wouldn't have been as vulnerable to parts ordering fallout when a new person started.

Another story that might resonate with the 3x5 card company would be if they were thinking about succession planning options. What if they were presented with a story about a similar company who also maintained their inventory on a 3x5 card system, but in this case, they were interested in selling the company. They figured they'd save the money and let someone else deal with the ERP upgrade. What they found was that their company was hard to sell. Investors and private equity funds wanted more turnkey operations, and there was too much risk with the file card system. When the company finally sold, it was at a discount, which was greater than the cost of installing an ERP system. Both of these stories attempt to draw the hesitant ERP buyer into the conversation.

By telling stories with real-world examples, the prospect can relate it to their situation, which helps move them through the purchasing decision.

When you use storytelling as an element in the engagement process, you're telling the audience why they should care. You're using a story as a bridge. Some stories may invoke empathy, like my Humane Society experience, and others may engender fear or even a shared vision. In all cases, you prepare the audience to embrace the next thing you have to tell them. A relevant story might be just the thing that makes your audience member think, "They really get me." It might be the presentation that makes the audience want to sign up for your newsletter or ask for a meeting. Because they see themselves.

Storytelling within the firm

Storytelling can be used in your internal communications as well. Professional service firms are filled with really smart people, but many of them are skeptical by nature. This can make change management difficult. Storytelling can help engage even the most reluctant of change agents.

Imagine you're talking to partners and staff about the need for them to get involved in practice development. They've probably heard this message countless times before, but what if you add a story that talks about the "why?" It might be a story that shares your desire to make more partners, showing how growth can create more space for the talented young men and women you recruit from college campuses each year and giving more folks the opportunity to earn a seat at the partnership table. No smoke-filled private rooms, but an honest and transparent approach for staff development at your firm. It's one thing to tell your staff that PD is important; it's another to use a story to show them why.

Storytelling can be especially helpful when you're trying to set a vision for the future and to give everyone a common goal, especially when the change you're driving is intangible and people can't envision it. I led an effort in 2009 with my marketing team concerning the adoption of a thought leadership program. We were a small team at the time, and we were at an out-of-office marketing retreat. Things had changed with the 2008 recession, and marketing was in a state of flux. I had a vision about how digital thought leadership could help us build an audience and nurture prospects. In an afternoon, I laid out my thoughts and told a story culminating in what I saw as the future "day-in-the-life-of-a-marketer" — and how that future could grow our firm.

Like all change, I first encountered pushback. There were dissenters — some people initially wanted to rework our old analog model, some were skeptical, and others couldn't see how the vision would tie into everything else we were doing. We spent the afternoon considering everyone's opinions and made a list of challenges to our vision. I knew that I had to get the marketing team on board or I'd never get the partners they work with on board. (I couldn't have my marketers saying to the partners, "Antaya wants us to do this thought leadership thing, and I think he's crazy, but I promised him I'd talk to you about this.")

Instead, we made a list of challenges, put together teams to address them, and created a story that eventually inspired the marketing team — and then the partners they supported — to join the vision. Our program became very successful, but it started with a story, a vision for the future.

Conclusion

Storytelling gives us the best opportunity to engage others in your vision for the future. It's also a great way to better understand your prospect's point of view and thought process.

If you're thinking the story will help them relate and it doesn't, that may be equally beneficial, as you've now uncovered obstacles you weren't aware of before.

If you're hiring marketing team members, make sure they have a skill in this area, and work with your existing team to close any gaps they may have. It's the difference between being lectured to and having a meaningful two-way conversation. It may be the bridge you've been looking for to close your communication gap — and eventually new business.

GET OFF OF THAT DINOSAUR!

These tips will help you get out of The Stone Age and into The Digital Age:

- Consider adding a story to an upcoming communication, and measure the response compared to your average engagement statistics.

- When you're meeting with a prospect — especially at that all-important second meeting — consider introducing your thoughts based on stories of how you helped clients with similar challenges instead of just touting solutions.

- Use storytelling to inspire your staff and make them willing ambassadors for change.

See Tool 13 in the appendix for a generalized model of an annual internal communication calendar.

26

Happy Clients Are the Point.

Happy clients are the reason you get to stay in business and the key to attracting more clients. But how do you evaluate their satisfaction that's meaningful to your clients, prospects, and staff? You need a system that's independent and actionable.

This was a challenge we faced at Plante Moran. Our system using paper surveys showed that our clients were extremely happy, but our partners weren't comfortable talking in the superlative about results from an internal survey. So we implemented an independently administered and compiled survey from a firm that focused on client satisfaction research.

This was a game-changer for us. Our staff, clients, and prospects found a common language to talk about our satisfaction in a way that was factual and objective. No one at the firm could be accused of exaggerating the data since it was independently reported by experts. The research firm administered surveys for thousands of companies across multiple sectors. This gave our staff, clients, and prospects a variety of reference points when evaluating Plante Moran's client satisfaction. It's one thing to say our clients are happy;

it's another to be able to provide data that they're happier than other familiar organizations.

Now, initially I did get some pushback from partners who didn't think we should publish results if they were less than 100%. But nobody's perfect — and with scores regularly topping best-in-class organizations like Amazon and Apple, those folks came around pretty quickly.

In addition to the benefit of getting accurate measurements, this approach elevated our standing with prospects and clients as a firm dedicated to client satisfaction and process improvement.

A client satisfaction measurement system should include feedback on a project basis as well as feedback targeting C-suite leaders on the overall relationship. You don't want to be in a position where the project manager gives you positive feedback and then be surprised when the C-suite wants to replace you because they're unhappy.

Project surveys

Consider creating a self-administered project survey that's distributed by the engagement lead at the end of every project. This should be a centralized system available to project teams yet maintained at the organization level.

The project survey should gather macro and micro feedback on the project team. You don't want to burden your clients with writing your staff performance reviews, but their input can give firm leadership more insight into what transpires when you're not around. Generally, the project survey should measure satisfaction with the overall deliverables and engagement process. Like an NFL football team on any given Sunday, there may have been a win, but each team member may not have contributed equally. Since your staff performance management system includes client service and feedback from client evaluations (if it doesn't, it should!), the project survey is a reliable and objective route to gather this feedback.

From time to time, your team may get negative or constructive, project-level feedback. When ratings fall outside an acceptable range, your process should include a built-in escalation step. You don't want your client team to rationalize away the negative feedback without someone from management getting in the loop. If there are actions that are causing client dissatisfaction in one engagement, there's a chance they're happening on others. You need to know to take corrective action and make sure your clients feel heard.

Sometimes, clients want their feedback to remain confidential. On both project surveys and overall surveys, I recommend that you allow the client to provide confidential feedback that's only seen by firm leaders — and maintain that confidence.

Relationship surveys

There are many ways that professional service firms evaluate their overall client service and different ways to use the data. You need to decide what's best for your organization.

Considering that client satisfaction is such an important measurement of your client promise and such a fantastic tool to tell your story to prospective clients, I find it astounding that many professional service firms self-report their client satisfaction measurements or use generalists who don't have a focus on client satisfaction.

If you're like me, when you make purchasing decisions, you rely on independent quality reviews — so why wouldn't you set up a similar system?

I recommend a robust survey — as many questions as you can fit into three or four minutes on all the areas that can impact satisfaction. At a minimum, a robust client satisfaction measurement system should include the following:

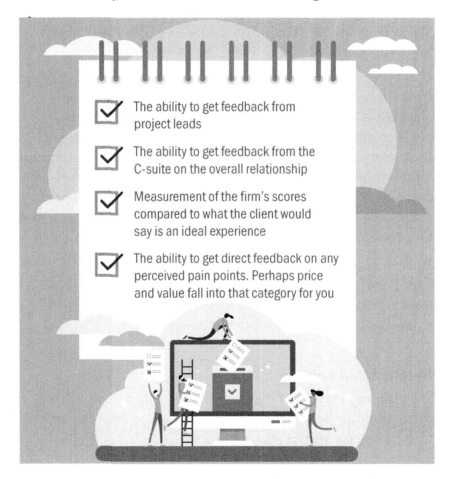

- ✓ The ability to get feedback from project leads

- ✓ The ability to get feedback from the C-suite on the overall relationship

- ✓ Measurement of the firm's scores compared to what the client would say is an ideal experience

- ✓ The ability to get direct feedback on any perceived pain points. Perhaps price and value fall into that category for you

PRICE AND VALUE — A TOUCHY SUBJECT

Price and value are important pain points, but talking about them is often taboo. You might think that if you don't mention price and value, the client won't think of it as an impediment. Your clients are increasingly sophisticated buyers, and they want great service for the fees they pay you. Don't hesitate to include a question about price and value in your client survey. It caused a lot of trepidation when we added the measurement at Plante Moran, but the data was useful.

Frequency and other touchpoints

How frequently should you survey your clients? I suggest the following:

- Project surveys should be sent after every project.
- Client satisfactions surveys should be performed by an independent firm at least once every two years — and consider offering them to your top clients annually.

For top clients, it's important to schedule an in-person meeting to discuss the results. I recommend making sure a member of your leadership team can attend. Some firms also include the engagement partner, and some have even added a "Chief Client Experience Officer" into the mix (often a retired partner, marketing team alumni, or practice staff looking for a new opportunity). The goal is team-building and transparency — with the added benefit of additional assignments that often come to light during these discussions about how your firm can continue to help these clients.

One data point that can provide great insight is asking first-year clients how their experience compared to what was described in the selling process. If there are gaps, you want to know for future r eference and to repair any damage that may have resulted. Your investment in first-year clients is real, and you don't want to throw it away due to a misunderstanding. If the experience turned out to be better than presented, you want to know that, too. You may have been underselling your firm, so you'll want to revise your RFP responses and present data proving that new clients experienced better service than was promised or explained in the proposal process. Wouldn't that be refreshing!

We've explained why the client satisfaction survey process and results should be a big part of how you describe what it's like to be your client in your proposals. This same information will also help when making outreach to referral sources. As we've said, a good professional will only refer your firm if they believe you'll take as good of care of their clients as they would. Independent data to support your claims of satisfied clients is a huge factor in gaining referrals. It can also be a factor in getting internal referrals from your partners, especially at larger firms where not all partners know each other.

Summary

It's one thing to have satisfied clients; it's another to have documentation of that satisfaction. Consider an independent program designed to protect — and perhaps also boost — your reputation in the eyes of your clients, prospects, and staff.

A great client satisfaction score should be celebrated. Thank your staff, and tell your clients. Make sure they understand you're taking their satisfaction seriously by setting up in-person meetings to discuss the results as well as opportunities to continue to serve them going forward.

GET OFF OF THAT DINOSAUR!

These tips will help you get out of The Stone Age and into The Digital Age:

- Periodically share your client satisfaction process and results with your clients.

- What's your client participation rate? If it's low, consider:

  » Notifying participants that the survey is being issued and explain the importance of their involvement.

  » Promise confidentiality to participants.

  » Offer a donation to a charity for participation.

- Create a rapid process for management to quickly identify and debrief on poor scores.

- If available, compare your scores to companies considered best-in-class. Look for opportunities for improvement.

- Get feedback about the client satisfaction content used in proposals from friendly business owners who aren't clients.

.

27

Marketing's Role in the War for Talent.

In any organization — but particularly professional service firms, wealth management firms, and not-for-profits — success will always rest on the quality of the people on the teams. You can bring in time-saving technologies and install AI software, but those don't power growth — people do. That's why it's so important to use every available tool to win the perpetual war for talent.

I didn't initially understand marketing's role in the recruiting effort, but I came to my senses very quickly when realizing that job seekers regularly ranked second or third when it came to plantemoran.com visitors. This will likely be true of your organiza-tion as well — and it's marketing's job to make sure your websi can attract the best and brightest out there.

Your website as a recruiting tool

In much of this book, we've talked about how the website uld engage prospective new clients — the same approach ne to apply to recruits as well.

Your website should list open positions, but if that's all it does, you're missing the boat. It needs to tell the story of what it's like to work at your firm and address the workplace issues that your target recruiting personas care about most. (Your HR team can help here.)

That said, be careful of trying to be too "hip." At Plante Moran, we once worked with an agency to create a "cool" look targeting college recruits. We modeled our approach after the recruiting pages of other firms, and we didn't focus on whether the recruiting brand was consistent with our firm brand.

The following year, we did a focus group with some of our summer interns. They reviewed the site and told us they noticed the lack of consistency between the recruiting pages and the rest of the website. They worried that this disconnect signaled that the recruiting effort wasn't incorporated into the firm and didn't represent what they'd experience when they joined us. This was a great lesson; just because other firms were taking this approach didn't make it right for us. More research would have steered us away from that misstep.

Speaking of research, it's a useful discipline to identify all of the decision-makers in the recruiting process and make sure you address their unique needs. Some of your audiences will likely include:

- College students
- People currently working in fields where you consult
- People working at competitors
- Children of your clients and referral sources
- Current staff
- Parents of future employees

You may be thinking, "Parents? Really?" Yes, really. Ignore them to your detriment. Helicopter parents are real and only becoming more influential. If fact, they may be sitting in the lobby right now while the college student is interviewing at your firm!

Once your audience is defined, your job is to create a path designed to encourage recruits to fall in love with your firm and the opportunities

228

you offer. Each group will want to be able to easily find and review your job openings in their area of interest. Tell stories about your culture. Talk about career opportunities. Share client satisfaction data and comments. And make it easy for them to apply.

It's also a good idea to periodically review your competitors' websites to see how your story compares to theirs. Like I said earlier, you shouldn't try to emulate them too closely, but if they have something that's appropriate that you forgot to address, by all means, add it to your story.

THOUGHT LEADERSHIP MIGHT ATTRACT EXPERTS TO YOUR FIRM

Some of the high-quality thought leadership you've generated to attract prospects may also attract the interest of highly qualified talent in those fields. Even though the readers may not be actively in the job market, the exposure may pique their interest where none existed previously. If you can get them to raise their hand and consider the possibility while they're on your site, you may have an opportunity to get them to join our team.

Finally, in addition to optimizing your website, you can use digital advertising to supplement your efforts, especially in highly competitive fields. Consider a retargeting advertising campaign aimed at those who viewed your job openings. Advertising could also include pay-per-click or ads on recruiting sites, internet searches with your competitors' names, geofencing at recruiting events, and referral source email campaigns.

Summary

When it comes to recruiting, marketing can be an invaluable partner to HR. Make sure your website tells a compelling story — one that job seekers simply can't ignore. And consider supplementing those efforts with digital advertising. The war for talent rages on; it's important to make sure you're highlighting everything that makes your firm stand out from the rest.

GET OFF OF THAT DINOSAUR!

These tips will help you get out of The Stone Age and into The Digital Age:

- Track the sites where your job seekers originate: Google, LinkedIn, Indeed, etc.

- Track the number of visitors to job postings compared to applicants.

28

I Heard It Through the Grapevine.

It's said that every organization has a culture, and leaders set the tone. No matter what type of culture you have, I'm willing to bet that internal communication plays a role in it.

Internal communication can help determine how engaged your employees feel, how much they trust your leadership, and ultimately how successful you'll be in implementing the initiatives that you adopt. It's a leadership strategy that factors into every business objective your firm undertakes, and the form it takes, the methods you use, and the intended audience all factor into its effectiveness.

Face-to-face communication is rare these days, so firms are increasingly reliant on digital tools to convey important messages to their teams. These tools tend to be one-way and don't encourage the type of give-and-take that's the basis for effective communication. It used to be said that employees' most preferred communication method was to receive important messages from their direct supervisor, but today, many messages come via email or through shared employee portals. These can be a poor substitute.

Let me ask you a question: How often do you get frustrated because someone on your team isn't aware of information that's been communicated? All the time, right? But do you ask yourself why? Why aren't your employees reading your messages? Since it's our job as leaders to ensure our audience reads our messages, you probably need to go to greater lengths than you originally thought.

The professional communicators on your marketing team can help. They can help you:

- Create a firmwide internal communications strategy and editorial calendar.

- Craft compelling messages. Storytelling can be beneficial here.

- Distinguish between various audiences — and target communications accordingly.

- Determine an appropriate frequency of communications — and make sure leadership communications don't overlap with other internal communications, creating "noise."

- Determine what methods are most effective for various communications — and allow for two-way communication, as appropriate.

- Measure effectiveness. (You'll be able to tell who's reading your communications, who's not, and who's opted out altogether.)

A well-thought-out internal communications strategy combined with a good technology platform can keep your employees informed, on board with what your firm is trying to accomplish, and offer thoughts on how they can contribute.

When working with your marketing team to develop your internal communication protocols, consider these questions:

- Do our multiple audiences need different methods of communication? (Probably.)

- Do firm leaders get a heads up on important communications, or does everyone get them at the same time? (I've always found it's best to communicate important items to firm leaders first — that way, if staff have questions, they're not caught off guard.)

- Do we have a standing communication plan for the items that happen every year?

- Do we have forums for two-way communications with our staff?

- Are our people held accountable to know the information we've provided them?

- Do we repeat messages, or do we tend more toward a "one-and-done" approach? (Spoiler alert — repetition is your friend. According to guerrilla marketing techniques, a consumer needs to see an ad nine times before they buy an item, and only one out of three ads register. You can apply this logic to internal communications, too.)

- Do we review the effectiveness of major communications to look for process improvements for the next one?

- Do we have tools to identify who's read our communications? Is there a plan for people who habitually don't read them?

- Are we focused on content length and engaging titles to help with readability?

- Are we educating new employees about recent policy updates effectively?

- Are our communications written to advance change? (Is there a separate document to fulfill legal obligations?)

- Is management realistic about the number topics requiring understanding over a fixed period of time (month, quarter or year)?

- Are we avoiding peak times of client responsibilities? (For example, at Plante Moran, we avoided putting critical communications out between February and April 15 due to tax season.)

- Do we have our eye on the prize? (Communications should be more than checklists for management, HR, and IT. They should support change efforts and help position the firm for long-term success.)

- Are we effectively using summaries to complement longer, more detailed communications?

Summary

Good internal communication is a science, and it requires discipline. It can be aided with the right tools that fit with your workforce's lifestyle. It requires creativity, reinforcement, listening, and accountability. As a leader, you need to lead by example and use informal channels to reinforce important messages.

GET OFF OF THAT DINOSAUR!

These tips will help you get out of The Stone Age and into The Digital Age:

- Internal communications is a field of its own and is important to your firm's success. If your internal team doesn't have the right skills today, hire a consultant to help them learn.

- Change management specialists aren't usually well-versed in good communication practices. Make sure you have both change specialists and communications team members on your project teams.

- Challenge the status quo about when communications are issued. Fiscal year-end and the beginning of the calendar year are often peak communication times. Can some of those communications be spread out throughout the year instead?

- Make sure you're using communication platforms that resonate with your audience(s).

- Ensure that communications are saved in an orderly manner so that staff can return to them later. Similarly, if a communication becomes obsolete, make sure there's a process to delete it to avoid clutter and confusion.

- Designate a day each week when significant communications are released, so everyone knows to look for them.

- Develop an annual calendar for important firmwide communications so everyone agrees with the schedule and has an expectation of when items will be issued and updated.

29

Alumni, Client, Referral Source — All Blended into One.

Professional service firms are among the few professions that prioritize remaining on good terms with their alumni. This is because these former staff often become prospects, and you never know when they might become the decision-maker who advocates for or against your firm for a new project. Alumni also make valuable referral sources. Even the person who appears inept to you today could move into a position of power tomorrow. So keeping touch with these folks is a good idea.

Maximize your alumni database

To keep in touch, you need to prioritize obtaining the personal email addresses of departing staff. All too often, this request is just one line item in a sea of line items that staff are asked to complete when they leave — and oftentimes, it's overlooked altogether.

Sound familiar? If so, you may need to reengineer how you collect post-employment contact information. What if you were to create an incentive for the departing staff to provide their information? While I've never seen an incentive system in use, I think it would be an inexpensive way to capture valuable information. Your firm could give each departing staff member a $100 gift certificate as a thank you for all the hard work they contributed while they were at our firm — emailed to their personal address 10 days after their last day. Bam! You'll get those emails for sure! And while it may take several years for these investments to pay off, all you need is a couple alumni to hire you for significant jobs to make the expense worthwhile.

The next suggestion may sound simplistic, but I guarantee it's not. You need a database system to tag your alumni and their contact information. A CRM system is the best option, but whatever you use, it should be cumulative and have good archival rules.

While some firms have robust HR systems, they don't always do as great a job of tracking previous employees as they do current employees. If you're using a cloud-based HR system, for example, you might encounter fee pressure to keep your storage small, so older records are deleted. Moreover, there's a temptation to limit costs by bringing over the minimum number of files during system conversions. Don't let this happen to you. Consider the lost opportunity when a third-year staff leaves your firm and, 15 years later, they're in a position to hire your firm — but they've vanished from your alumni database. CRM systems are designed to accommodate long-term prospecting efforts and may be the best system for your alumni-tracking efforts.

Make them feel special

As part of your marketing efforts for alumni, start a club. Perhaps you produce a quarterly or semiannual newsletter that features brief updates about the firm and their fellow alumni. You could include a longer interview with a successful alumnus (this is a great business development opportunity as well) and include general interest or hot topics like artificial intelligence or the tax impact of employee stock options. You could also include job openings to lure lost talent back your way. (We had a lot of these "boomerangs" at Plante Moran.) Bottom line: You need to treat alumni as a "persona" and include content that they want to read.

But sometimes a newsletter isn't enough to keep this audience engaged. That's where an annual alumni event comes in. This event can generate ongoing engagement and goodwill by offering the opportunity to catch up with old friends. Done right, it will become something everyone looks forward to each year.

I would invite every person who previously worked at the firm (including support or non-client servers) back for an evening. Be sure to include a liberal number of current staff at all levels, including your support teams. If funds are limited, don't cut down the guest list; throw a cheaper event. Hold the event from 5-7 p.m. on a Tuesday, Wednesday, or Thursday evening. No speeches or agenda, just a gathering of friends and acquaintances to keep your firm top of mind even without any direct marketing messages. Inviting everyone may cause some initial consternation, but I meant it. If anyone left on bad terms, chances are they won't come if there's still bad blood.

Here are a few final thoughts for consideration:

- The annual cadence is important. Why? Because if the cadence is erratic, people won't know what to expect— and attendance will start to dwindle.

- When you're starting an alumni program, consider creating an incentive to encourage participation. For instance, offer one Thanksgiving dinner for a person in need for every alumni who attends. Be sure to give this offer prominent placement in the invitation.

- No matter what your budget is, make the event impactful.

Conclusion

Your firm's alumni are among some of your best new business opportunities. Too often firms don't realize this until years after alumni have left their employment. Be conscious of the future potential of this group, and create a program today. You might even try to recruit some high-profile alumni to help you plan the program.

 GET OFF OF THAT DINOSAUR!

These tips will help you get out of The Stone Age and into The Digital Age:

- Create a report that highlights the percentage of personal email addresses obtained from departing staff.

- Send a letter from your office, or someone on the leadership team, to the personal address of each departing staff to thank them for their service. If no personal email is provided, be proactive about getting them.

- Consider creating a program to encourage alumni to refer you new business. It can be as simple as dinner for two at a local restaurant, but it will keep the idea of referrals top of mind with this valuable group.

My Last Word.

Last summer, I was hosting a birthday dinner and wanted to serve a champagne cocktail. I looked for a recipe and was shocked at how many options I found. How could there be so many recipes for a simple champagne cocktail?

Like any good host who wanted their guests to enjoy the start to the evening, I decided to pre-sample the recipe I chose before the big night arrived. I recruited a friend, and we mixed up the selected cocktail as prescribed. After tasting it, we made a few adjustments based on the food being served and the preferences of the birth-day honoree. These tweaks resulted in a customized, one-of-a-kind cocktail that was specially designed for our guests.

Why am I talking about cocktails? In this book we've covered many of the elements that will produce a successful marketing campaign for professional service firms, wealth management firms, and not-for-profit donor programs, but like my cocktail recipe, there isn't just one path to success. A successful program depends on the ingredients and the team trying to accomplish the goal.

In my example, for the best outcome, it wouldn't make sense to hire someone to craft a specialty cocktail who'd never had cham-pagne before or had never paired champagne with food. Marketing efforts are similar — you start with a good mixologist, have quality ingredients, a good recipe, and then you adjust to individual taste.

Although you may get a good first attempt, award-winning results happen with a system of process improvements that finds the right mix for your firm.

At Plante Moran, I was fortunate to work with a team who usually had a fantastic first effort, but that was never enough for us. We set a high bar and continually challenged ourselves to test the upper limits. At times it was scary, but we always gave it a good shot, and we always surprised ourselves.

Your success going forward will depend on five things:

- A very capable marketing leader and with a strong team

- A strategic marketing plan that acts as a roadmap

- An integrated marketing plan that uses multiple tactics

- Open-minded leadership who are unafraid to try new things, reward good attempts, and understand that mistakes are the tuition for experience

- Commitment to continual process improvement

The last point is especially important. Earlier in this book, we acknowledged that, like an iceberg, success is more than just the deliverables produced. The performance statistics that most people don't see are the ones that help drive future efforts.

In my role as the marketing team leader, I was responsible for creating the marketing vision, leading execution, building firm consensus, and learning from our own experiences. These were big responsibilities, and I wouldn't have been successful without the help of my team and partners. I pride myself on exploring the edges of the new, but I relied on our team and other thought leaders to help lead our journey. I needed to paint the vision of how our marketing tactics would work together for my team and the partners. I needed to close any gaps our team had to achieve the vision and show the path to success.

You probably have many of those same challenges. If you have doubts at any step along the way, use an expert to help you navigate the pitfalls by creating a growth path you'll be proud to have as your legacy. Creating synergy between your marketing resources and your partners that optimizes growth and creates a positive environment of shared respect is a wonderful goal.

I love helping organizations tailor a marketing plan with tangible growth expectations — there's no greater reward than making this journey with firm leaders who have a similar vision. This book was never intended to be a "how to" book but more of a survey of options. If you need help to interpret the best recipe for your firm or want a "second opinion" about modifications you think are necessary or even an independent evaluation, contact a marketing professional who knows professional service firms. I love this work and would love to help you, but there are also many other talented people out there who can help. Whatever you do, act! Get off that dinosaur, and get with the digital age.

APPENDIX

Tool 1:

What to Include in an Orientation Program for Referral Sources and Business Developers

Be sure to share:

- The story of how the firm was founded.
- Your client service philosophy.
- Client service results.
- Client retention rate.
- Industry and service areas where you specialize.
- Community and industry awards.
- Conferences attended and presentations given.
- Board positions of partners.
- Associations where you belong.
- Any conflict policies to express that you won't steal clients from referring organizations or say anything negative about referring organizations.
- The onboarding process for new clients.
- The client satisfaction process to get clients' ongoing input.
- Any process to satisfy an unhappy client.
- Any referral programs.
- The much sought-after businesses you'd love to have as clients.

Tool 2:
Guide to Develop a Model Persona of Your Ideal Client

The more information you know about your targets, the better chance you have of attracting and nurturing them. Here are a few areas to understand before developing your plan:

- Industry where they work

- Average age range

- Associations where they might belong

- Titles that they might identify with (for example, CEO, Partner, CFO, CIO, Chief Legal Counsel)

- Size range of companies or families that you're interested in working with

- Likely hobbies (golf, tennis, equestrian)

- Other service providers who are likely to also be attracted to these prospects

- Influencers to this segment

- Primary source of news

- Strong religious or ethnic affiliations

- Other dominant traits or traits that aren't incidental, like common software systems, common employment challenges, etc.

- Items they may collect. (art, cars, coins, etc.)

- Volunteerism possibilities

- Interests your targets may have outside their work role (retirement, education, aging parents, etc.)

Tool 3:
Process to Create a Marketing Job Description Tailored to Your Firm

- Define the goals for the marketing team and its leader. (Creating a job description without knowing the goals and requisite skills is a recipe for turnover.) This includes targets for:
  - » Revenue
  - » New clients
  - » New cross-serving opportunities
  - » New team capabilities
  - » And more
- Quantify a goal for each bullet above after one year and after three years.
- Identify the required skills to meet the goals.
- Identify relevant backgrounds that may help the candidate be successful.
- Establish a salary range.
- Establish a budget for the marketing team to meet the stated goals, and make sure there's alignment between goals and spend.
- If necessary, enlist outside help to ensure the best outcome.

Tool 4:
Sample CMO Job Description

Chief Marketing Officer

Your role.

Your work will include, but not be limited to:

- Operating as an in-house captive marketing agency to help create brand recognition.

- Creating a strategic marketing roadmap to keep a competitive short-term advantage, with a foot in the game on investing in the right strategies for long-term market leadership.

- Leading and developing a team of marketers to provide the best marketing solutions to business challenges we face in an ever-changing environment.

- Creating and supporting processes to keep the firm's investment tools and digital assets up to date.

- Leading and executing internal communication and PR strategies, using newsletters, media, press releases, publications, and PPC and SEO.

- Leading the team in optimizing a heavy event and trade show selling environment.

- Engaging in competitive intelligence research, gathering, and analysis for use in strategic planning, firm positioning, and business development activities.

- Guiding the efforts of the pursuit and proposal team to ensure optimization of opportunities, and create industry-leading, winning proposals and RFPs.

(continued on next page)

Tool 4 (continued)

- Leading firm efforts to track and analyze business development progress and results and provide regular reports to firm leadership from CRM.

- Preparing and managing business development and marketing budgets, as well as monitoring and controlling department expenditures accordingly.

The qualifications.

- Bachelor's degree in marketing, business, communications, or related field; MBA preferred

- 15+ years of business development/marketing work experience and proven success in professional service organizations

- Strong skills in developing people in a quickly advancing digital field and distributed team environment

- Professional marketing and business development network

- Strong experience and proficiency in Microsoft Office (Word, Excel, PowerPoint, Outlook, CRM), and other technology platforms, including marketing automation, websites, and social media

- Strong leadership, collaborative, and consensus-building skills to work closely and successfully with staff, managers, clients, and vendors

- Strong project management and event planning abilities, including demonstrated ability to multi-task, prioritize, analyze, organize, follow through, delegate, and negotiate

Tool 5:
Sample Marketing Scientist Job Description

Marketing Scientist

The basics.

The Marketing Scientist is responsible for data analysis and measurement practices, allowing us to connect the dots between the online and offline behavior of our buyers and those who influence the buying decision. They will develop buyer insights with actionable implications, integrating research into all phases of marketing planning process. This work is central to our digital marketing initiatives.

Your role.

Your work will include, but not be limited to:

- Designing and developing methodologies and approaches for new measurement solutions that inform the buyer's journey.

- Identifying and applying appropriate methods and approaches to measure the impact of marketing on buyer behavior (e.g., purchasing, sign-ups) and client outcomes (e.g., incremental revenue), including designing complex experiments.

- Analyzing and synthesizing extremely large first-party and third-party data sets into easy-to-understand insights and measurement solutions.

- Serving as a thought leader and advisor on measurement approaches, methodologies, and KPI development.

(continued on next page)

Tool 5 (continued)

The qualifications.

- Bachelor's degree in mathematics, economics, statistics, behavioral science, or other quantitative field

- 7+ years of analytics experience; advanced degree in quantitative field may substitute for 2 years of experience

- Expert knowledge of analytical or statistical techniques

- Experience with experimental design and/or AB testing

- Experience with advanced experimental and quasi-experimental design approaches and analytical techniques

- Experience in SQL

- Project management skills and experience necessary to work autonomously and manage competing demands across multiple teams

- Comfortable delivering analytical presentations and story-telling insights to non-technical audiences and stakeholders

- Experience building explanatory or predictive models

- Experience building data visualization in Tableau

Tool 6:
Outline of a Successful Interview Process

- Armed with your job description, select job boards and associations to post your open position.

- You'll get a mix of people who apply with varying qualifications, so before you post the positions, create two screening questions to highlight the best candidates and identify unqualified candidates. Screening questions usually have short, quantifiable answers. Potential screening questions might include:

  » Number of people managed

  » Number of digital campaigns managed in the last year

  » Revenue of current employer

  » Number of new leads in the last year

  » New revenue or leads from digital sources

  » Current email platform or current CRM platform

- Based on the job description, create 10 interview questions that can be used by the interview team.

- Ask HR or an outside consultant to review the resumes and perform telephone screens on candidates who best meet the requirements, and have appropriate responses to the screener questions.

- Select five to seven candidates for in-person interviews.

- Before their in-person interview, create a "case study" about a problem they may have to face if they join your company. Ask them to bring their solution to the in-person interview.

(continued on next page)

Tool 6 (continued)

- Allow them to present the case study to you. This can provide great insight into the person and their skill set.

- Using the predetermined interview questions, arm each member of the team with 3–4 of the questions. This way, you'll get broader insight into the candidates rather than creating a situation where interviewers may repeat questions.

- Allow time for the candidate to ask questions. The quality of their questions can provide great insight. No questions or poor questions should send up alarm bells.

- After the interviews, the team will debrief and select the top 2–3 candidates for follow-up interviews.

- In the follow-up interviews, review the job goals and expected results that were prepared in advance. Get input on the goals and the opportunities and challenges that the candidates see. For challenges, ask them for proposed solutions.

- Once the final interviews have occurred, make a decision.

- Be sure to engage a marketing professional throughout the process. (Other professionals might be tricked by inappropriate marketing buzzwords or jargon.)

Tool 7:
Potential Interview Questions for Marketing Leaders and Staff

- Tell me about a time when you needed to convince a client (internal or external) about a new marketing idea. How did you construct the conversation?

- When selling audit services, which are often a necessity mandated by banks, what do you think our approach should be to open the door with new prospects?

- Tell me about a time when you personally identified a new approach or technology that could help the organization better identify or attract new business. How did you introduce it to your marketing colleagues?

- Tell me about a time when you had a staff person who was doing their best to support the team, but their contribution was significantly less than most other members. What did you do?

- How do you help your managers keep focused on their "A players" and not get sidelined with performance issues from less talented team members?

- Give me an example of when you had to jump into a role where you weren't totally comfortable but had to demonstrate leadership. How did you handle it?

- How is social media used at your current company, and can you quantify if it's led to new business?

- Tell me about a time when you were surprised at a buyer's journey that was different than you expected.

(continued on next page)

Tool 7 (continued)

- Tell me about a time when you were part of a new client pursuit team. What was your role in the process?

- Tell me about a time when two of your direct reports had a difference of opinion. How did you resolve it?

- How would you go about identifying ideal client profiles and making sure people throughout the firm were in the know?

- Success at a professional services firm is a tailored combination of marketing tactics, messaging, and practice staff business development efforts. Can you give me an example of how you helped to move the needle in this area?

- Tell me about a time when you had to prove the value of a large marketing investment to a colleague or client who didn't have a good understanding of the marketing function. How did you approach it, what was the outcome, and what would you do differently if you had a do-over? (This is similar to your first question, but in this case, it's not about a new idea but justifying the company's spend on marketing overall.)

- Give me an example of a time when you initially vetoed a marketing idea or implementation by one of your staff members but eventually changed your way of thinking. (This speaks to the candidate's ability to take input that may differ from their own and learn from it/compromise/ grow or admit to being wrong.)

- How do you motivate and reward your staff, particularly during times of high change/stress? Give me an example of this in action.

Tool 8:
Case Studies for Marketing Candidates to Demonstrate Skills

- The organization has identified family offices as a potential client/donor. Devise a plan to develop this new audience from initiation to new client/donation.

- The firm has decided to implement a scoring model to notify them of interest from their most promising prospects. Create an implementation plan that highlights the opportunities and the pitfalls.

- The company has set a goal to increase business from existing clients. Create a one-page plan to meet this goal.

- Referral sources are an important source of new clients/donors. The organization believes that a more formalized approach would result in even more new business. Devise a one-page plan to help us reach our new goal.

Tool 9:
Sample Business Developer Weekly Meeting Agenda

Before the call, ask the business developer to prepare a simple report that lists the following (usually based on a week or two-week period before meetings):

- Number of cold calls made
- List of prospects where the first conversations occurred and the outcome
  - » Added to CRM
  - » Added to LinkedIn connections
  - » Offered company subscriptions
- Prospects with a planned second meeting
- Proposals in process
- Events attended
- Referral sources contacts
- Internal meetings
- Prospects contacted where no follow-up meetings are currently scheduled
- Invitations for any upcoming events where the business developer is currently recruiting attendees
- New events that could be planned to help the business developer with their sales goal

Tool 10:
How to Develop Business Developer's Compensation

		Example
Targeted total business developer compensation (1)	$ XXX,XXXX	$ 400,000
Multiple factor for minimum sales quota in Year 3 (2)	4–6	4
Total revenue from new customer from BD (3)		$1,200,000
Quarterly revenue target in Year 3 (4)		$300,000

Calculation of split between base and commission

If annual sales target is:	$1,200,000
The commission for Year 1 and 2:	
Commission for Year 1 (1,200,000 * 10%)	120,000
Commission for Year 2 (1,200,000 * 5%)	60,000
Total commission	180,000
Required base to reach $400,000 (5)	220,000
Total compensation (Year 1 and Year 2 commission plus base)	$400,000

(continued on next page)

Tool 10 (continued)

(1.) Total compensation needed to attract an experienced business developer with a proven history of attracting $1 million a year or more.

(2.) The revenue is four to six time that of total compensation in Year 3.

(3.) Total revenue in any year should be 10% of first-year revenue collected and 5% of Year 2 revenue.

(4.) No commission paid until the YTD commission target is met.

(5.) In this example, we backed into the required base if you agreed to pay $400,000. However, you can adjust this number up and down if you want to pay more or less. If you want to pay your business developer a total of $300,000 for sales of $1,200,000, the $220,000 would be adjusted to $120,000.

Tool 11:
Sample Integrated Marketing Plan

Goals:

- Increase revenue from new clients by 10% from prior-year growth rate.

- Develop family offices executives as a new client segment.

- Increase revenue from existing clients by 10% over the prior-year growth rate.

Tactics:

For this example, we'll create a plan around the firm's expertise in cybersecurity as a lever to attract new audiences and upsell current clients.

- Create three pieces of thought leadership.
    - » Five dangers of cyberthreats most organizations get wrong (article, five paragraphs)
    - » Three protections you need to know about in a cloud computing world (infographic)
    - » What your family doesn't understand about cyberthreats (2-minute video)

- Identify 2-3 speaking opportunities at trade shows or family office/family business conferences.
    - » Use the thought leadership as a post-event follow-up.
    - » When a piece is opened and read, follow it with a second piece.
    - » When two pieces have been read, offer a free, 15-minute consultation.

(continued on next page)

Tool 11 (continued)

- Use LinkedIn to create a targeted ad campaign where the thought leadership pieces are offered.
  - » Test which does the best job of identifying new audiences.
  - » Nurture readers with the other thought leadership.
  - » When anyone has read two pieces, offer a complimentary, 15-minute conversation with one of the authors.
- Contact local business publications, radio stations, newspapers, and TV media about interview opportunities concerning cyber-security for the family.
- Watch current events for significant cybersecurity incidents and offer up firm experts for commentary.
- In month seven, create a list of questions that clients and prospects asked, and develop thought leadership about frequently asked questions.
  - » Distribute to people who accepted the 15-minute consultation but didn't purchase your services.
  - » Create a webinar and invite everyone who's clicked on any of the articles.
  - » Allow attendees to request a 15-minute, hassle-free, private follow-up.
- Create a tailored piece on cybersecurity for your referral sources that they can use to engage their clients — and hopefully bring you new business.
- Develop a pipeline of opportunities, and devise a conversion plan for highly desirable targets:
  - » Ask referral sources for introductions.
  - » Use LinkedIn to find common connections who can help.
  - » Assign "sales" team responsibilities for a more personal interaction.

Tool 12:
Content Health Check

- Is the topic included in a Google search of things important to your target audience?

- Does the title convey an urgency to the reader?

- Do you signal to the reader that they can complete the article in an acceptable period of time (five things you need to know, the ABCs of..., the best five minutes you can spend on cybersecurity, etc.)?

- If content is longer than five paragraphs or extends more than 3 minutes in a video, can you break it into sections?

- Do you use images and infographics to tell the story and emphasize messages?

- Do you offer the reader multiple ways to:

  » Subscribe to similar content?

  » Ask to speak to an expert?

  » Offer feedback?

- Does your software have the capability for readers to share with others?

- Once published, are readers staying engaged until the end of the article? If not, how can you improve the abandonment rate?

- Is there a "short-form" option that can be used to engage new readers and a longer version to nurture known audiences?

Tool 13:
Sample Internal Communication Annual Calendar

Regular and consistent internal communications build a foundation of trust between leaders and their teams.

The following is for illustrative purposes:

January
- Happy New Year message
- Outline of goals for the new year

February
- Affirmation of firm's commitment to diversity and the impact on improved client service

March
- Look back at the accomplishments of the prior year

May
- Results of the first quarter
- Memorial Day holiday message

July
- Fourth of July message

(continued on next page)

Tool 13 (continued)

August

- Progress in the first six months toward the annual goals
- Thank-you message to team members who have made outstanding contributions
- Welcome to new team members who joined since the beginning of the year

September

- Labor Day message
- Client satisfaction results

November

- Thanksgiving message
- Review of the first nine months

December

- Holiday message

Made in the USA
Monee, IL
28 June 2021

71976814R00154